A HEALER'S JOURNEY

A HEALER'S JOURNEY

Sree Chakravarti

Rudra Press

Portland, Oregon

Rudra Press
P.O. Box 13390
Portland, Oregon 97213
800-876-7798

Illustrations: Hannah Bonner and Laura Santi
Photographs: Rupinder Khullar and Olaf Hauge

Printed in the United States of America
Cover design by Bill Stanton

Chakravarti, Sree.
   A healer's journey/Sree Chakravarti.
      p.   cm.
   Includes index.
   ISBN 0-915801-39-6 : $16.95
    1. Chakravarti, Sree. 2. Medical personnel, Ayurvedic — India —
Biography. 3. Healers — India — Biography.   I. Title.
R608.C47A3   1993
615.5'3'092—dc20
[B]   93-1865
                                          CIP

The book is dedicated to Sai Baba of Shirdi, *the saint who has inspired my healing and whose power guides my hand;* and to my dear husband, Satyandranath, who died *before my book could be published and whose love and encouragement I miss most deeply.*

CONTENTS

**PART TWO: A Practical Legacy — Self Healing
        Techniques and Remedies**

ACKNOWLEDGEMENTS

I believe I would never have written this book without the encouragment of two very special friends, Tara Ali Baig and Margaret Beveridge.

Tara Ali Baig, the well known Indian writer and social commentator, first suggested I should write when I told her about my visit to Saudi Arabia to treat the Saudi royal family. Shortly before her death, I sent her a few of the first pages of this book for her "honest opinion." She wrote me a beautiful letter, giving me so much encouragement that I took my writing seriously for the first time.

My dear friend Margaret Beveridge, the Canadian film maker, had wanted to make a film about my healing practice ever since our first meeting. Perhaps it was not God's will. All the film she shot and all the tapes of her interviews with my various patients were lost in an accident. She was so very sad, but from the time I showed her my first chapters, she became very excited and enthusiastic about this new project. When I was not in the mood to write, or not sure of my work, she was the force making me continue. She was a friend and guide, a benevolent mother, who sometimes praised, and sometimes scolded, but always her love overflowed her criticism. Today, when I finished the book, I wished so much I could show it to her, but sadly fate decreed otherwise. Her death will always be a great sorrow to me.

I also want to thank my dear friend, Veronica Hauge, for offering to edit my work. I have no words to thank her or do her work full justice.

Before her magic touch, my book was like a flower without fragrance. I take her editing as a grace of God, and for the grace of God, one can only be thankful to God who bestowed that grace. So I leave it at that, praying to God to keep her healthy, to give her peace and bliss, and a long and happy life with her husband.

I must also thank my friend Joan Ames for her additional editing of my book and for the changes she suggested to make it more lively and interesting.

EDITOR'S NOTE

Sree Chakravarti's account of her healing in this autobiography is so simply stated and matter-of-fact that it is perhaps easy to lose sight of the miraculous quality of her work.

As a frequent visitor to her home, I have witnessed, over and over again, the transformation of those who come to her for help.

To take one example — a young military officer who has flown to Delhi from army college in South India. His problem: a slipped disc so agonizing he has had to request leave of absence from this critical training. With him is his father, a retired army officer, painfully proud of his son, so fearful of his future. The son sits in obvious pain, tense and anxious while we wait for Sree to finish treating her current patient. Now Sree shepherds in an elderly lady. "Sit, rest, relax a few minutes. Do you need a taxi?" Sree settles her down, then bustles off to call the taxi and to wash her hand to clean and cool it. When she comes back, the father leaps to his feet, his son pushes himself up with his cane. She questions the young man briskly while his father hovers beside them. Finally she says, "Come, let's have a look at you," and the young man hobbles after her to the treatment room.

We all sit while the father seeks reassurance from Sree's kindly husband, a retired army colonel, who presided for many years over the drawing room where we wait. For distraction we look at the birds fluttering over the feeders set out each day on the balcony by Sree. Within ten to fifteen minutes Sree and the young man return, the son smiling and walking much less stiffly. Again the father leaps to his feet, "Will he be all right?"

"Look at him, what do you think? Of course, he's already much better, but he's got to drink *kulthi* water three times a day, and drink at least eight glasses of water to loosen up his system. Come tomorrow at the same time. What do you owe me? Nothing! Nothing! My healing is a gift from God, how can I charge?"

Now it's my turn. What is a healing session with Sree like? Sree's healing room doubles as her dining room, a single bed at one end is where she heals. The treatment end is filled with pictures and statues of Sai Baba of Shirdi, the Indian saint Sree believes gives her the power to heal along with bookshelves crowded with ayurvedic texts. Sree describes in her book how she uses her right hand to diagnose, how her hand starts vibrating spontaneously, indicating with extraordinary accuracy the site of the problem. During the actual healing treatment, it is just Sree's fingertips that touch the patient, and her hand will work gently over a particular area of the body until the vibrations stop of their own accord.

But this treatment is no hushed, mystic, spiritual experience. For a moment, before she starts to treat you, Sree will sit quietly, her face turned away as she takes a deep breath to center herself and concentrate her powers, but while her hand vibrates, she will chat about everything under the sun, smiling and laughing. Her servant of many years, Mungal Singh, will come to fetch something from the refrigerator. The phone will ring and Sree will toss a message for the caller over her shoulder, all the while, her hand vibrating on your body.

If this is your first treatment, imperceptibly you begin to relax, to trust, to believe in the unbelieveable — that this amazing woman's hand *can* cure — an extraordinarily difficult concept for anyone only familiar with Western medicine. In my case, I was intensely sceptical until I was actually treated. But after treatment I did not really need the confirmation of a reassuring CAT scan from Yale/New Haven Hospital. Deep inside me I knew I was better because more even than the bodily healing, Sree heals the spirit, restoring to one a faith in life's order and completeness, a will to live.

Perhaps you will think the example of the young military officer — who was able to rejoin his course within less than a week — no more or less convincing a cure than one a skillful chiropractor or physiotherapist could achieve. But what of the patient I met who had been crying for eight years without stopping? The first day the middle-aged woman came she sat and wept in the drawing room, a picture of total dejection. Her friend explained she'd begged her to come to Sree when she'd heard doctors in London and New York had been unable to help. When this patient emerged from Sree's treatment room — on her very first visit — she was transfigured, unable to stop smiling. She could hardly believe that her tears had stopped! Sree herself was laughing. "Isn't it amazing, I can hardly believe it myself. I've never heard of such a thing, such a strange condition."

Sree is now in her late sixties, with a body kept young by yoga — she can uncurl into a head stand or bend over to place her hands flat on the floor without a moment's hesitation. She is not tall, yet seems so because she is so youthful and erect. Her hands, on which she wears several rings, are as small as a child's but possess incredible strength when she is working. Her dark hair is graying and she often wears it loose over her shoulders. She always wears a sari and around her neck a chain with a medallion of the old Sai Baba, the saint of Shirdi.

Sree is very open to everyone and her expressive face radiates genuine concern, an old-fashioned motherliness. It is hard for her to judge, dislike, or criticize. As she says, "I look for the light in people, not the darkness." She is genuinely unimpressed by wealth or influence and she treats all her patients equally whether they are cabinet ministers, rich industrialists, young clerks, or taxi drivers. Everyone who comes to her feels they have made a friend for life and many keep in touch for years, whether or not they come for healing. She has in abundance the gifts a true healer needs: love, compassion and spiritual awareness.

Sree has been described as "a simple Delhi housewife" by one of her great admirers, the late Tara Ali Beg. In a sense this is true as Sree always had enormous concern for her late husband and the smooth managment of her household. It is also an indication of Sree's essentially mysterious quality. On the surface she appears an unusually friendly, almost ordinary person. She makes no cult of herself, she is very matter-of-fact about her powers which she explains as magnetic vibrations. Yet underneath she is deeply spiritual with strongly held beliefs, in awe of her own essentially unexplainable gift. Could she ever imagine a time where she would not heal, I asked her. Her answer was an immediate "no."

To those who know Sree it is almost unbearable to think she is unable to hand on her healing gift. In this book she has not only given us an account of her life of service, but has also done her best to leave behind a detailed, practical legacy of the herbal cures and exercises she uses to augment her healing. She recommends only those treatments she knows from direct experience can help, in the hope that with care and diligence many sufferers will be able to help heal themselves.

— Veronica Hauge
Westport, Connecticut
U.S.A.

FOREWORD

Much has been written about spiritual healing, and yet the scientists are, for the most part, unconvinced. If I were reviewing the literature without any personal experience of it I would also be among the sceptics. But that is no longer the case for me since meeting Sree Chakravarti in New Delhi, India, more than twenty-two years ago.

I was serving at the time as the Canadian High Commissioner to India and Ambassador to Nepal. I had developed a growth on my right shoulderblade about the size of a golf ball, and my whole body felt threatened by the tumor. I was ill in body and spirit. About a month before I was to undergo surgery, Sree began treating me. While I lay face down on a couch in her New Delhi home, she passed her right hand over my back without touching me. As it came to the growth, her hand began to vibrate violently, returning to normal as it moved away. I could watch her in the mirror. On the mantle below the mirror was a postcard of Sai Baba — not the one now living, but the Indian saint of the last century at whose tomb in Shirdi thousands of pilgrims still come each year to be healed. Each time her hand passed over my right shoulderblade I could feel a definite surge of warmth around the growth, as if a deep-heat, infra-red light bulb had been turned on and off. From the time of my treatments until my operation, I experienced no more concern and my body felt once more in its normal wellness state — not under attack as before. When the biopsy was done after surgery, my "golf ball" was diagnosed as a non-malignant lymphoma.

It makes no sense to my mind to say that Sree changed a malignant growth into a non-malignant growth, but that is how it felt to me; and since my feelings and my mind continue to cohabit the same body, the question remains open to this day.

My experience is what the medical profession calls "anecdotal," inconclusive, not of any real scientific value. But it is not alone. Sree has effected many hundreds of cures as convincing or more convincing than mine. And Sree is not alone. Throughout recorded history people have been healed by a "laying on of hands," by touch, or by an energy passing through the hands into the affected part of the sick person's body. Of course there have also been thousands of pseudo-healers living off the gullibility of the ill, who hope beyond hope for a miracle.

What is the reality after discounting all the illusions? I think those willing to bring an open mind and heart to the enquiry will find in Sree's account of her own work as a healer several valuable clues to the mystery that inevitably remains — inevitably because we are dealing in all probability with the action of higher levels of reality upon our three-dimensional world. The modern mindset is not comfortable with the notion of "higher levels of reality." Our consciousness is only now emerging from a mindset (or paradigm) framed by a Newtonian world view in which all the clockworks operate on the same mechanical level. From what we now know of the very small- and the very large-scale worlds around and within us, we begin to acknowledge that there must also be a quantum reality whose laws are different. Perhaps sometime in the next century we will be waking up to the reality of mind, of consciousness, of conscience, and of love at the root of our being of all that is. Only then, it seems to me, will we be on the track of a real understanding of what actually happens through rare individuals like Sree who are, in a way that will be forever mysterious, able to channel energies we can only call Higher. Yet even today these are the energies in which we "live, and move and have our being," as St. Paul put it a long time ago. That contact happens to us throughout our lives, automatically, like our contact with the air we breathe. When we are ill it may often be that something has interfered with that contact and we may need help in getting it started again, in the way that mouth-to-mouth breathing can revive a person who has nearly drowned.

From Sree's account of her experience of healing one thing is dramatically clear: the power refuses to flow through the ego. If a healer's success creates fame, money, or power that goes to the ego and supports the feeling "I did it," that healer will soon discover that he or she has lost the gift of healing. The power is rigorous in its requirements. Without an egoless state, nothing will really flow. I suppose it was for this reason that Sree decided to destroy most of the records she had been keeping of her many cases. Better to have the power than the fame, which can always be seductive. Even the greatest healer knows that the power must be served, not commanded; that it is unquestionably higher. Those who forget this, lose it.

Seen in this perspective the life of a healer is necesssarily a life of practice and service; "not my will, but Thine be done," as Christ said in his suffering. When the suffering and the service are conscious, miracles can happen. But the healer feels this egoless state must be maintained with constant vigilance or the ego will take charge again and the connection will be lost. It is "every moment Zen." Healing can only take place Here and Now while the healer's state is pure. On the relative scale, that is true for each one of us, not just Sree. Each of us may aspire to heal one's own self, as the first step towards being able to help others.

Sree, I thank you for your healing and for the love that makes it possible for you to heal.

— James George
Port Murray
U.S.A

A HEALER'S JOURNEY

Sree at age 23, after her marriage in 1947.
The photo was taken by her husband.

PART ONE

The Journey

An Account of a Life of Service

MY PRAYER

This is my prayer to Thee, my Lord:

*Give me the strength to make my life fruitful in the
service of others, and give me the strength to surrender
to Thy will with love.*

— Rabindranath Tagore

I feel that my voyage is soon coming to its end. For this I must write
what I want to say. Some inner force is compelling me to write about
myself and about all the patients I have treated. Nobody will ever know
them the way I know them. For me they are not ordinary people — they
are like a bouquet of flowers of different hues and fragrances. They have
transformed my life.

My ambition in life was to become the mother of my children. Today,
I am known as the mother of many different people. They belong to
different castes, creeds, and nationalities. God has fulfilled my desire to
become a mother, only I could not become the mother of my own child.

Oh, King of Kings, come and take charge so that I may write. God,
you have coloured me with the speck of dust of Your feet and honoured
me with a right hand that heals by touch. The hand is mine, but it is Your
power that heals. It is You, not I.

1
AN INTRODUCTION
TO MY BOOK

It has been very difficult for me to write this book. I have never written anything before and I am always very busy with my healing work — and sometimes very tired — but so many of my patients and even doctors and other healers have asked me to leave some record of my work. Also, although I believe my healing is a gift that I cannot teach or hand on, I have been urged to make a list of the natural cures and yoga exercises I recommend in conjunction with my healing. My only fear is that some readers might misunderstand and think I am trying to advertise myself. I hope it will become clear in the course of the book that this is not the case. Over the more than thirty years I have been healing, I must have treated more than thirty thousand patients. I still have too many patients and many more are waiting to see me.

Always when I meet someone new, I am asked about my work — how I diagnose illness, how I do the treatment, what I can cure, have I had any medical training. I have had no medical training, but after working for many years with so many patients and doctors, I have acquired an understanding of the body and how it works. I discovered my gift slowly, and I am still finding out areas where it will heal, but I have been very successful with the following problems: slipped discs, spondylitis, ulcers, blood clots, some heart problems, over-activity of the thyroid gland, kidney troubles (except kidney failure), brain injury, and any wounds that fail to heal in any part of the body. I have also been able to heal a number of strange and unusual cases that had mystified the doctors or been declared incurable.

It seems my hand is not effective if the whole body is under attack, as in a massive stroke, or in illnesses like cystic fibrosis, multiple sclerosis, muscular dystrophy, or Parkinson's disease. For the same reason, I find it very difficult to treat cancer patients if the disease is too far advanced, or if they have had chemotherapy or radiation, which destroy the immune system. This is because one of the ways I work is to activate the thymus gland which I believe controls the immune system. If my hand can restore activity to the thymus gland, it can restore health to the entire body. In fact when my hand vibrates on the thymus gland, I know from a certain subtle difference in the current passing through my fingers if the immune system is under attack. When the attack comes from cancer the vibrations on the thymus seem to go much deeper. I can no longer accept cancer patients. It drains too much of my energy and so often a cancer cured in one part of the body will surface in another.

Three other areas I do not treat are asthma, skin problems, and any kind of mental illness. In the case of mental problems, it seems that if I cannot make a true contact with the patient's mind, it is hard for me to heal. It makes me very sad to have to refuse or turn away any patient but I cannot cure the whole world and I believe I am better to save my energy for those problems I know I can help.

People are always interested in how I do the actual diagnosis and healing. I examine patients when they are lying down — if in my home, on the same bed where I do the healing. During the diagnosis, I move my hand slowly down the body, starting at the head, and holding it about six inches away. Some sort of an electrical field is built up and my hand vibrates most strongly at the actual site of the problem. This vibration is completely automatic. My theory is that sickness is caused when electrons in the atoms of the ailing area act abnormally. It seems my right hand possesses some kind of magnetic vibration and I believe this vibration, or radiation, helps to adjust the electrons and create a magnetic field that balances the body. This is only my theory, but somehow I feel it is the true explanation. Why my hand should have this power only God can say.

For the treatment, I usually see a patient for about half an hour, two to three times a week. Each treatment ends when my hand stops vibrating. Sometimes it will vibrate longer, sometimes for less time.

Sometimes but not always patients will feel heat or vibrations or a shock during treatment or lassitude after being treated. Always I ask them to rest a little time after treatment in my sitting room.

My own hand always feels very hot during and after treatment, often as if it were burning up. I always wash my hand after a sitting, in part to cool it. All treatments take some energy from me. I don't normally allow people to touch me, and I have to stop myself from spontaneously embracing people which is my nature. Somehow I am afraid too much touching, except in healing, will interfere with my powers. I have also been warned never to allow anyone to try to measure my vibrations with any kind of electrical experiment because it might damage the delicate electrical impulses coming from my hands.

I know after two to three treatments if I can help a patient. It usually takes ten to twelve sittings for a patient to be cured, even though he or she may feel much better after the initial treatment.   Sometimes it takes much longer to be sure a patient is really well, but that is now more unusual as my power has been increasing each year, and it seems to be increasing faster all the time. I can't explain everything to a logical mind, but certain things I know absolutely, even if I cannot explain them.

When I talk of "my" hand like this, I particularly want readers to understand that I don't mean to boast of "my" powers — it is not my hand that heals, but God's. All the times I have been healing I have had to guard against a feeling of pride in "my" work or boasting about "my" powers. When I first discovered my gift and I was puffed up with pride about myself, I started keeping a record of all my cases, what dates the patients came, what was wrong, how long it took to cure them, and so on. One day I decided it was only foolish pride, that I might lose the gift if I boasted about it or thought, even for one minute, that it was "mine." What is the need of records, except for my own ego, when my hand will tell me whether I can heal or not heal? Our ego is the dust on the mirror that prevents us from seeing God in ourselves. I must never forget that I am the glass, not the water in it.

I have been asked many times how I prepare myself to heal. I do not know if I would be unable to heal if I did not meditate, but I start each day with yoga breathing exercises, followed by fifteen to twenty minutes of meditation. I did not always do this. When I first discovered I had the gift, I was ill myself — sometimes I was so sick I could not walk five steps. I decided then that if I were to heal others, I must get well myself. Slowly, slowly, I started doing yoga and slowly I built up my strength.

Often when I meditate, I find that problems connected with a patient's health will come to me and be solved. I believe it is also during my period of meditation that Sai Baba, the saint of Shirdi, may come to me and help me. I would like to sit much longer in meditation, but always I am too busy. In addition to my healing I am also a housewife with a home and all its duties to care for.

Another question I am sometimes asked is what part my own religion plays in my healing. I am a Hindu, that is the religion in which I was brought up, and I worship Krishna and the Mother in all her forms — Durga, Kali, Saraswati, Mahalakshmi — but I do not believe my religion as such is involved. When I go into any religious structure — whether it's a temple or a mosque or a church — it's very strange but my whole body vibrates like a stringed instrument. When I am asked about religion, I answer, "There is one God, does it matter whether one drinks from a glass or a cup?" Surely, one of the saddest problems in today's world is all the growing religious intolerance.

I am also asked if I am a "spiritual" healer. I believe that my power to heal comes from Sai Baba, the saint of Shirdi. It does not matter to me or to my healing whether or not the patient believes in my powers or in Sai Baba. If the patient can be healed by me, my hand will heal him whether or not he believes in me, that is the strange part. Another strange thing about my power is that I can use it to heal myself, almost as if the power were independent of my own body. I don't really feel though that my power should be used for myself, except that I need to be well to have the strength to heal others. I understand St. Bernadette, the patron saint of the great healing center at Lourdes, when she refused to bathe there, saying, "It is not for me."

Spiritual healing is by its nature holistic healing. In treating people I find that a great deal of illness is associated with the mind and I never treat only the body. Normally I like to talk to my patients at the same time I am using my hand to heal them. I find that as soon as I touch my patients, they have a sense of comfort and they relax. It is then that I try to find out if they are suffering from any tensions or mental anxieties.

I remember one particular case: a very beautiful woman had married a man who seemed not very handsome by comparison. She was also very clever and had helped her husband build up a business empire. Without realizing it, her husband had developed an inferiority complex and had become more and more tense when he was with his wife. Finally he consulted me for what he believed were physical problems no doctor could diagnose. As soon as I put my hand on him, I realized that there was nothing wrong with his body, but while I vibrated my hand on his head, he poured out all his feelings to me. I told him there was nothing wrong with his body, that his trouble was only in his mind and that he could cure himself by learning to relax through meditation.

In my experience these factors above all underlie problems of physical and mental illness: greed, hatred, pride, envy, and lack of insight. By my touch and in talking to my patients, I try to understand their problems and suggest to them in a mild way that they try to change their attitudes by relaxation and meditation. This is what is meant by holistic healing.

I have included some of my dreams elsewhere in the book. All my dreams are so vivid and clear cut, it is as though they are actually happening and sometimes they seem to have special meaning or to have pointed the direction for my life and healing.

One of the strangest and most wonderful dreams of my life came soon after I'd started healing. In this dream, I see myself as a Christian father who is even younger than I was at the time, very tall and handsome, with long hair coming to my shoulders. I am wearing a gown of the most beautiful blue I have ever seen. The gown is tied with a silken braid at the waist and I have a rosary of small beads around my neck. I am moving from bed to bed in a hospital, advising the two nurses working there what to do with the patients. The nurses are dressed like saints in the Jain religion. When I go outside I see rows of men standing on either side of the road to greet me and in the crowd a few women in saris with cloth masks to cover their mouths. When I woke up, I wanted to close my eyes again, the dream was so happy and so real. I can still visualize the whole scene clearly.

In another vivid dream that I had at about the same time: I am walking up up to the top of a mountain. The small piece of cloth I am wearing just covers my body. I am following a tall old man while far below I can see my husband, my father, and some of my relatives. I am not sad to be leaving them behind. The old man looks back to see if I am following. "Don't look back," I say, "I am not properly covered." "What," the old man shouts at me, "after all my teachings you are still aware and conscious of your body." He speaks so harshly I get frightened and wake up. I wonder, was the old man Sai Baba? Will I ever meet that person in real life?

Another dream I remember very clearly also came to me early in my healing. I am standing on a balcony and nearby is a river and a temple. I cannot see anyone but someone is telling me to go and worship. "You don't need anything," says the voice, "only your devotion is the offering." Then the voice continues, "Just look at that child walking on the water, he is going to the temple and his devotion is so strong he does not sink." I look and I am not surprised. Then I find myself inside the temple and there is a raised platform on which there is a picture covered in red hibiscus flowers and, nearby, a tray holding more of the red flowers. I examine the picture but find there is no image, only the word DEVOTION in bold gold letters on a red background. Now I ask someone who has appeared if I can buy a red hibiscus flower. I give him money and he gives me sweets and a white flower. "I don't have any more money, how can I worship if I don't have the red flower I asked for?" I am begging and crying. I woke up and found tears pouring down my cheeks.

Several years later I went to Calcutta and visited the famous temple of Mother Kali. Suddenly, on a balcony, I saw the same raised platform as in my dream and beyond flowed the river. Later I was told by an astrologer that I am "part of the mother" and that I should worship Her, as well as Krishna. He said I would increase the power of my hand by worshipping the Mother because she symbolizes *shakti* or energy.

The same astrologer gave me a book in Sanskrit called *Durga Sapta Sati* (The Description of Mother Durga in 700 Lines), which describes in verse how Mother Durga was created by all the Gods to destroy the demon. He told me that reciting the verses or *slokas* in this book would help me awaken my own *kundalini shakti*, the mysterious energy that lies coiled at the base of the spinal column. Once awakened it can destroy the evil in us as Mother Durga destroyed the demon, and by achieving this power, we can do good to others. From that day I have worshipped the

Mother as well as Krishna. I've often thought that perhaps that early dream about the red hibiscus was telling me to worship Mother because the red hibiscus is Mother's flower.

Another dream I first had when I began my healing but which I see very often, again and again, still today: I have entered a room where there is a small raised platform. Sometimes it is a big room, sometimes small. Sometimes it is very bright there, more often it is in semi-darkness. But always there are many garlands and flowers and there is incense burning. I see no one there. I feel someone is going to worship, but there is neither priest nor image. When I open my eyes, I can still smell the lingering fragrance. I have dreamed this dream again and again.

Another question I am often asked is whether I was ever given a sign that I would be able to heal before I began my work. I believe I was given two signs when we were building the home in which I now do the healing. While the house was under construction, China invaded India in October, 1962, and my husband, who was a lieutenant-colonel in the army at the time, was so busy at his office that I had to supervise all the work myself. One day when we had all the preparations made for finishing the roof, Delhi was threatened with unexpected heavy rains that would have set back the work several months. When the storm came it rained so much all over Delhi, except just the small area near our house. It seemed as if God wanted the building to go ahead.

The second sign came a little later. When our house was almost finished, I was standing on the roof directly above the room where I now heal. At the time ours was the only house with more than one story for some distance around. It was a still evening. Suddenly a little card drifted down from nowhere and landed at my feet. On it was a picture of the Virgin Mary with St. Bernadette. I couldn't imagine where it could have come from, but I felt immediately it was something magical and meant especially for me. Before I had started healing, I'd seen the film about St. Bernadette five or ten times — I felt so strongly her work had something to do with my life. I still have that card. I feel sure it was a sign that I was to be a healer.

During my healing work, I have met all kinds of people, rich and poor. Sometimes I feel riches and power are a terrible handicap. Many rich people think they can buy the world with their money. How foolish.

One very rich man from Kuwait boasted to me, "I can buy anything I want with my money, only name it."

"If you think you can buy everything, then why are you sick? Get well with your money, I will not treat you," I told him.

Another very rich man I treated had many many friends. When he came for treatment he insisted on knowing about my fees. "You cannot pay, I don't accept money or gifts," I said, "Does God charge us for the sun's rays, how can I charge for His healing?" My patient got very angry. He kept insisting and insisting he must pay, so I finally said, "All right, this is my payment. When you get well, you must not tell any of your friends how you got cured."

"But how can I not tell them?" he said. "That's really impossible!"

"I know," I said, "that's why I told you that would be my payment." Only then did he understand the joke.

I have called my book "A Healer's Journey" because I feel my whole life since I knew about my gift has been like a voyage of discovery. First I found Sai Baba of Shirdi, then He showed me I could heal and still today I am discovering new powers for my hand. Along my journey I have met so many pure and noble souls through my healing. I cannot forget any of them and whenever I feel lonely or depressed I remember their wonderful qualities. I think of them as a garland of flowers to offer at the feet of God in thanks for their filling my empty heart with love and compassion.

Each day I pray to God, "Let my life be like a candle which will burn near your altar to the end. And let my body become like incense that will give more fragrance the more it burns. You have touched my body with Your grace, and the body which is made from dust turns into sandalwood with Your touch. From nothing You have made me something for Your service. Let me not forget, even for the flicker of a second, that without Your grace and love, I am a cipher."

2
CHILDHOOD

From my childhood, I was prepared for this healing work. I believe it was what I learned then about sharing and service to others, and the deaths of my mother and grandmother when I was still very young, that shaped my life forever. Preparing to write about those days opens the door of memory and brings back those times to me as if they were yesterday.

I grew up in a large joint family household in Bhagalpur, Bihar, where many people were given shelter and all were brought up in the same manner. We had everything we needed, but no luxuries.

The head of our joint family was my grandfather, Charu Chandra Bose, a learned man and a famous lawyer. He was a very busy man and the whole household was in the care of my grandmother, Firoza, who had been born and brought up in Ferozpur. My grandmother was also a well known social worker. I remember she ate only once a day, at midday, and then only when all the family had taken their meal, including the servants. She would then put on a white sari with a beautiful colored border and go out to do her social work.

Our family were followers of Mahatma Gandhi and active in the movement to free India from Great Britain. My grandmother was in charge of a school where ladies and young girls learned to spin flax into thread. The thread was used to weave the plain *khadi* cloth worn by followers of the Mahatma as a protest against the import of British textiles.

My grandmother was a strict disciplinarian. She would stand no nonsense from anyone, at home or in the school. She was such a strong person that everyone was afraid of her. In addition to care of the household and her social work, from time to time my grandmother went to Burdwan, some one hundred and fifty miles away, where the family owned landed property. There she sorted out and settled problems. In accordance with the Mahatma's wishes, our grandparents gave away many acres to their tenants.

My father, Mon Motho Nath Bose, known at Mani Bose, was the eldest son. He had two brothers and three sisters, but as they had all been born much later he had been very pampered when he was young. He was employed as an aerial photographer in the Civil Service and was often away. (I was to learn later that his service to the British was a source of some friction in the family.) He was also a gifted amateur musician, artist, and actor.

I was always very close to my father, particularly when I grew older, even though he was very strict with me. He was someone who would always answer all my questions and whose liberal opinions encouraged me to think for myself. "Look into your own heart, my child," he would say to me. "Don't care what the world will say. Keep asking yourself if what you are doing is right and you will find the answer in your own heart."

My mother, Torulata, was very beautiful and much younger than my father. She was a gentle person and always spoke very softly, but I don't remember ever seeing her smile. As the wife of the eldest son she was in charge of all the cooking and other duties of the household. We had many servants, but my mother had to be in the kitchen from early morning until late at night. My sisters and I had very little direct contact with her and were brought up by an old Bihari woman we all loved.

I was born on Sunday, April 25, 1926, at 4:30 in the afternoon. My parents already had three daughters and the whole family was very keen for the fourth child to be a son. As in Bengali custom, my father's father had named us children. My grandfather had given all my three sisters born before me names beginning with "s." The first sister, a four-syllable name, Shakuntala; the second, a three-syllable name, Savitri; the third, a two-syllable name, Sati. I was given a one-syllable name, Sree, to symbolize I was to be my parents' last girl child. One of the meanings of *sree* in Sanskrit is energy. It seems my grandfather had chosen a truly prophetic name for me.

I am told that when I was born, no one in the family rejoiced, and from the tender age of three, I was sure that I was not loved by anybody. They all behaved as if it was my fault or my mother's that I was not a boy. Perhaps because of this I was very lively, mischievous and naughty. I could not sit still a moment. As a result I was always in trouble and always being scolded.

I remember one time when I was about three years old I was playing with a small pencil that I pushed inside my nostril. I felt breathless and started crying. The whole household gathered round and someone ran to get the doctor. I was very uncomfortable, but what I saw made me wonder about being so sure I was not loved. Everyone in the family was upset and my mother was crying. We had a large garden the doctor had to cross to reach the main house. As he pushed open the garden gate, I sneezed and out came the pencil! The minute it came out, they all stopped crying and started to scold me. Still, I can remember so well thinking, if all these people don't love me, why are they all crying?

I remember another incident. My grandmother used to go early each morning by horse-drawn cart to the Ganges for her bath. Sometimes we had the good luck to go with her. After bathing, she would stand in the river to worship the Sun God and she looked so beautiful and serene, her whole sari-clad body wet and her black skin shining. She had the rounded body of a young woman that she kept right up until her death some years later.

One morning — I must have been five or six years old — I ventured out very early with one of my cousin-brothers to the river bank, quite a distance from our house. When we reached the river, it was much too early and only a few people were taking their baths. After walking some distance we decided to return. Little did we realize there would be such turmoil in the house. There were so many of us children, I had thought no one would notice our absence, but all hell was let loose. Every nook and corner had been searched and when the whole orderly house was in a mess, the children, with all the other family members and servants, had started searching the grounds. When they had not found us, all the children had started crying and all the adults were also in tears.

When we returned they were very happy to see us back. Again I asked myself the same question: Were they missing me, or were they crying only for the cousin-brother? But I knew they were crying for both of us. I wondered, if they don't love me, if they don't care for me, why were they crying? I felt truly sorry for having caused all the upset as I was the real culprit in this adventure. I was the only granddaughter to behave so badly. Even at that young age I was like a ball of fire.

3
TWO DEATHS

When I was seven years old, my youngest sister, Dhira, was born. We were now a family of six girls as another sister, Sujata, had been born two years before.

When the baby was just one month old, my mother became very sick. She had lost a tremendous amount of blood during delivery, and after that she developed severe anemia.

It is our Hindu custom to have a ceremony for the newborn when the child is one month old. I remember my mother looked very different, perhaps due to her illness. She was wearing a red-bordered sari with a red *tikka* spot on her forehead and her long silky black hair was floating in the air. I talked to her and she answered all my childish queries, but it seemed to me she did not belong to us anymore. It was the last day of her normal life. She became very sick and my little sister was taken care of by others. We were not allowed to disturb her, but we could see from a distance how she became thinner and paler. My grandmother was with her all the time. She forgot all her other duties and stayed with my mother day and night.

One morning I got up early and the house was very quiet. I ran to my mother's room. There was no trace of her left — no mother, no bed or bed table, nothing. The room was all washed and empty except for my grandmother sitting on the floor, weeping. I asked her, "Where is my mother?"

At first she did not reply, then she said, "Your mother is no more. She is dead. They have taken her to be cremated."

I could not understand. What was the meaning of the words "dead" and "cremated" and why was my mother "no more"? Then I noticed a huge basket of fruit on that empty washed terrace. "Who is the fruit for, grandmother?" I asked.

"It was sent by your mother's father," she told me between sobs. I can still remember thinking, my mother is no more, no more, now who will eat the fruit? Still, to this day, that huge basket of fruit haunts me. I cannot forget it sitting there for my mother who would never eat it. I fainted dead away and remained in a coma for two days. Afterwards, I was very sick for one month with typhoid fever.

Some time after my mother's death the whole family moved to Calcutta. My grandmother had lost all interest in life — she would sit quietly and weep the whole day for my mother, she could not bear her dying. She would take me on her lap and with tears running down her face she would tell me how she had first seen my mother at a marriage party. "Your mother was so beautiful, so charming. I knew from the first minute I saw her that she was the one for your father.

"When she came to our house as a bride, I promised her father I would look after her like my own daughter. Her mother had died, you see." Then she would tell me again and again, "I am responsible for your mother's death. I never bothered about her, I never gave her any love, I neglected her."

One day my grandmother fell down the stairs and was in a coma for one month. My grandfather looked after her as if she were a child. He would not allow anyone else to touch her except myself. I was only nine years old, but he used to ask me to sit near her and he taught me how to take her pulse. I don't know why I was the only one to be trusted. As I sat there, I used to imagine my grandmother was only fast asleep, that she would wake up and take care of everyone again. Such an active person lying like that. This lady, who looked after all the family property, who sheltered so many people, she who was like a queen, so fond of taking care of others, who all the time solved others' problems, what did it all mean? But I learned she had a brain injury and that the doctors could not help her. I knew now it was her turn, she was going to die, just as my mother had.

When my grandmother died I was near her. I saw when she stopped breathing and passed away peacefully. All her children were with her except my father. He could not come until a few days after her death.

Before the funeral, I knew I wanted to see everything so I would know what had happened to my mother. I saw how my grandmother was given a bath and dressed in a new sari. Her body was heaped with flowers and garlands and lots of vermillion powder was put on her forehead. Then, as is the Hindu custom, all the male family members and other male friends and relatives took the dead body in a funeral procession. I followed, keeping a little distance, and nobody noticed me. Suddenly they discovered me but I was allowed to go with them to the burning *ghat* by the Hoogly River and see my grandmother's body on the funeral pyre. I saw how our bodies slowly turn to ashes. I was standing near and slowly, slowly, the whole body turns to ash.

I started thinking, this powerful lady who was like a dictator, who was a terror to naughty children, gone and there is no trace of her. What is this life then? What is the use of all our pomp and show? However much we may take care of our body, it will turn into ashes one day. I wanted to ask so many questions, but who would answer my terrible need to know what happens after death? I wished my father were there to tell me. I still remember how grandmother's long curly hair, her face, everything, was slowly consumed by the fire.

God purposely wanted me to know about death. From that young age I knew the reality. However important we feel — comfortable, proud — one day we will turn into dust or ashes, that is the ultimate truth.

4

MARRIAGE AND HEARTBREAK

After my grandmother died, my sisters and I left the large joint family household in Calcutta and came to New Delhi to be with my father. We used to spend the winters in Delhi and the summers in Simla, when the whole government moved to the cool of the hills north of the capital.

Growing up under our father's roof, I continued to be the naughty one of the family. I was always getting into trouble — stealing my father's precious razor blades to hand out at school as pencil sharpeners, or racing about the house so fast I'd knock over and break all the china. My father would lose patience with me and slap me, but it would never bother me, and if I were ill he'd tell my sisters he missed the sound of my dancing feet. As I grew older I'd help him with his hobby of fretwork, and I was the one who knew where he kept all his tools and everything on his desk.

World War II came in 1939 and my father was more and more busy with his government work. We children went to school in Delhi and I was taught to read and write English, Sanskrit, Bengali, and Hindi as well as general subjects. I was always very good at sports. Although I would have liked to, I was never able to study science or biology. Looking back I realize a knowledge of those subjects would have helped me later with my healing. My father liked to entertain and we always had many guests. At a time when it was uncommon among strict Hindu families he often invited Muslim friends to dine at our home.

I continued to vex my father even in my teens. The independence movement was gathering strength after the war and one time I led all the pupils out of school to support the general strike called by the Freedom Fighters. "You'll lose me my job, you wretched girl," my father shouted at me. But I always knew he loved me and he would talk to me and answer with so much wisdom any question I asked him.

In 1947 India gained her independence from Britain and was partitioned into two countries, India and Pakistan. Terrible bloody riots followed and many tens of thousands of Hindus and Sikhs were killed fleeing Pakistan for India, and many tens of thousands of Muslims were killed fleeing India for Pakistan.

My future husband, Satyandranath, after serving in the Indian Army in the Far East, had been transferred to Delhi just a few months before the partition of India and Pakistan. We had first met when I was only sixteen and he had come to visit a friend at our house. Before I met him I was not at all interested in the idea of marriage — I was going to be a teacher. After meeting him, however, I thought that if I married, I would marry a man like him. We were married about five years later on my twenty-first birthday, April 25, 1947. My father told my sisters, "I have lost my right hand."

I expected married life to be quite different from what it was at first. My husband was an army captain and very busy with an important position in military intelligence. He got no leave and almost no time off. He worked on holidays, Sundays, and from early morning until late at night. Like my mother, I had married the eldest son and my marriage turned out to be an endless round of duties. At the time of Partition, his family had had to leave their happy protected life in Sind, escaping to India with only their jewelry. I, who had been so carefree and heedless, spent my whole time helping take care of all his people. I had no time to think of anything, it was only giving of myself. I had to arrange everything on my own; my husband and I never seemed to have any time to ourselves.

I never complained to him and in this way three years passed. Then the most wonderful thing in my life happened — I conceived, and the whole world changed its color. My dream of being a mother had become real. I gave up my studies for a Bachelor of Arts degree and my ambition now was to become the head of a large family, just as my grandmother had been. My cupboard was stocked full of beautiful clothes I'd embroidered for the baby we were expecting.

The delivery turned out to be very complicated. I was taken to a nearby nursing home where there were no arrangements for oxygen or other specialized facilities. I suffered terribly when I gave birth to our son and two hours later the child was dead. The inevitable had happened — I had lost the most valuable thing in my life. I had become a mother, but the son of our dreams was lost forever. With his death, a part of my life was dead.

I say "the inevitable had happened," because a few days before delivery I had a premonition that something was going to happen, some sort of misfortune was awaiting me. This might be dismissed as the natural fears of a young woman expecting her first child, but such premonitions have been true all my life and continue to be so even now. Before any unfavorable incident takes place, I become aware and start to feel afraid inside of me. Why and how I seem to know it beforehand I cannot explain.

After losing our baby, I was continuously sick for about twelve years — miscarriages, operations, all the time in and out of hospitals. I was warned by the doctors that I must not conceive unless I underwent major surgery. The military doctors had operated several times, but it had not helped. My only desire was to become a mother of our child at any cost. All the time I was praying, "Oh God, even if I have to die in childbirth, let me become a mother."

During this period we were stationed in several different places, but eventually we were sent back to New Delhi in 1961. Some years before, we had bought a small plot of land there where we now built our present home. I supervised all the construction because it was just before the war with China and my husband was too busy to leave his office. By then he was a lieutenant-colonel and had been given a very important assignment that kept him actively involved.

Although I was so busy during this period, I had stayed very close to my father and I was missing him very much. When the military crisis was over, I asked my husband if we could invite my father to visit us from Calcutta and bless our new house before we moved in. My father agreed to come which is how he came to spend the last month of his life with us.

During this last month, my whole life was changed by meeting a group of people who were all devotees of a great Indian saint, Sai Baba of Shirdi, who died in 1918. Just three days before my father's death, they invited me to a service for the saint. There was no priest or temple, we met in someone's home and all sang *bhajans* (hymns). The *prasad* (food first offered to the deity) given to everyone there was the simple food cooked in the house. When I came home I told my father how an extraordinary peace had entered my heart and touched me. I cannot even begin to say how important that meeting was to me, but I believe what I am today is all due to Sai Baba's blessing.

The day before his death my father was resting in the garden. It was getting dark. He called me to him and somehow he was different. "My child, my time is up," he said. "I don't have any more time at my disposal. I have been very bad to you. I did not realize who you are. I cannot rectify what I have done to you. I was always unkind to you."

I could not understand what he was saying. I didn't believe he was serious and I started to laugh. "I am your daughter," I told him, "and I used to be very very naughty, so it was natural for you to scold me and sometimes even slap me. Why are you saying you did not recognize me? What has happened to you? Are you in your right mind?" In my younger days I was used to his scolding, but now he seemed to be in some kind of trance.

"My child," he went on, "one day you will become famous. People will know about you from distant lands."

"Will I become so beautiful?" I asked him sarcastically. "Really, father, you are not making sense."

He paid no attention to what I was saying, he just kept repeating, "I made a big mistake about you. I am so sorry I did not know before who you are." Then he added, "But remember, my child, never put yourself higher than God, never let yourself become puffed up with pride, my daughter."

At the time, I had no idea what he was talking about. I thought he must just be very tired and I brought him tea and tried to soothe him. How I wish now that I had not laughed at him and called him foolish, but had asked him what he meant. The two of us were always so close, I have often wondered if perhaps at this moment — so near his own death — he had had a vision of me as a healer.

My father died on the stroke of three the next morning after suffering three heart attacks. By Hindu custom it is the eldest son who lights his father's funeral pyre, but our father had only six daughters. Because he had died under our roof, it fell to me to perform all the son's ritual duties at his death.

It is also our Hindu custom to cremate the body as soon as possible. After my father's body had been bathed and dressed and flowers had been brought to cover it, later the same morning my husband and I and a few friends accompanied his body to the burning *ghat* beside the River Jumna, holy to the Hindus because it later joins India's holiest river, the Ganges, at Allahabad. My father's body was laid on a bed of firewood and more firewood was placed on top. I then poured a small pot of *ghee* (clarified butter) over the pyre and put a lighted match to it.

We all stayed beside the pyre for the three to four hours until my father's body turned to ash. I then took a handful of the cooled ashes in a little earthen pot and went alone to cast them into the Jumna with offerings of fruit and flowers. This to us is the symbolic act of freeing the soul to go on its journey.

Three days after his death we held the *sradh* ceremony (last rites) in our home to pay respect to my father's departed soul and to pray for its peace. Family and friends were invited to a meal and offerings were made to the priest and food given to him to distribute to the poor helped by the temple. Even at that time, many families held the *sradh* ceremony in the temple, but we observed ours at home in the traditional way that my father would have wished.

Only a few days after my father's death I had a vivid dream. Remembering it still disturbs me, even so many years later. In the dream my father is standing in a roofless room, looking out at me from behind a barred window. My father is begging me to open the door and set him free. In the dream I tell him, "You are not my father. I myself lit the funeral pyre." He goes on begging me to set him free. I keep replying, "You are not my father." When I woke up from this dream, I felt miserable.

During the following months, my husband again became very busy at his office and I missed my father terribly. He had always been there to answer my questions, whatever I wanted to ask. Without him I felt I had no one to understand me.

In this anxious, lonely, disturbed state, I started to do a lot of thinking. I realized that after we were married, my husband had given me so much love I had changed from a mischievous young girl into a docile, loving wife. He had looked after me all the time I was sick, I had no reason to complain. But my only idea had been to please my husband and his family.

It was as if my father's death had awakened me from a deep sleep. I started asking questions of myself and seeing everything in a different way. The ground under my feet was not firm any more. I began to question all my values of unthinking service and obedience. From outside, nobody could see the change, but I knew I was changing inside. Slowly I was becoming a different person, consumed by the question, is there any meaning in life? It was then that I turned instinctively to Sai Baba for guidance.

5
SAI BABA, THE SAINT OF SHIRDI

Sai Baba was a real person — not a mythical or non-historical personality. The saint lived with us in flesh and blood in the village of Shirdi until October 15, 1918 — the day of the *Dushera* festival on which he took his *maha-samadhi* (left his body) at about the age of one hundred. He has been and still is the all-pervading living force that molds and transforms the lives of millions of his devotees regardless of their religion — Hindus, Muslims, Sikhs, Christians, and Parsis alike. Who was Sai Baba? What was he? What did he live for?

Baba's origin is unknown. He was given his name by Mahalsapathy, a devout Brahmin and custodian of the Hindu temple in Shirdi. When he first saw the saint he called him "Sai" and he became known as Sai Baba, Saintly Father. Mahalsapathy later became one of his closest disciples.

Sai Baba came to the village of Shirdi in the Ahmednagar district of Maharastra when he was a young man of about sixteen. He made his home under a neem tree and day-in, day-out he was to be seen sitting on a rock, meditating. To the simple folk who passed that way, he appeared to be mad. They did not recognize his greatness or divinity. He never asked for alms, but he did not refuse the villagers if they offered them.

The first time anyone realized Sai Baba was someone out of the ordinary came when a miracle happened. Some shepherd boys were playing under the neem tree where Sai Baba was sitting. Suddenly they saw a full-grown cobra with raised hood making a beeline for one of the boys. All the children ran, except the threatened boy, who was paralyzed with fear. Sai Baba looked up and saw the danger. A second before the cobra could strike, he gently upbraided the snake. "Why do you want to harm an innocent child? Please go back." The snake stopped in its tracks, glided to Sai Baba, dipped its hood in homage at his feet, then slid away. The children and two elderly men who had seen the whole happening told the villagers. From then on they looked on Sai Baba with new respect.

Soon after this incident, Sai Baba moved into a quiet corner of a dilapidated, mud-walled mosque he named Dwarkamai. He lived in the crumbling building with only snakes, bats, and owls for company. During the day, he continued to sit under the neem tree that he called his guru's place. During Sai Baba's lifetime, the spot was dug up at the saint's request and a tomb of two rooms with lights burning was found under the tree.

As Sai Baba became better known to the villagers he would sometimes ask for a little oil to burn in the lamps at his Dwarkamai. One day the villagers refused him. He did not reproach them, but in the gathering dusk returned silently to his crumbling mosque. A few curious villagers followed him and witnessed how he put cotton wicks in water and set them alight. Not only did the water burn, but the lamps remained alight throughout the night, spreading a heavenly glow. This was when the people of the village realized Sai Baba was someone divine.

Sai Baba never preached any religion. He never interfered in the religious practices of his devotees. The caste, creed, color, or status of his followers never mattered to him. He believed only in the divine law of universal love. Therefore he did not found any new creed or sect. His Dwarkamai was the meeting place for all religions. There Sai Baba taught his devotees the value of truth, the value of faith, and the value of love for attaining eternal salvation.

There was only one single thread running through all Baba's actions, his decisions, and all his words: His determination to help his devotees to rise above their ephemeral lives and to bathe in the immortal consciousness of the inner divine. He was the embodiment of the concept of universal love. As it is given by Krishna to Arjuna in the *Gita*:

> *I am the same to all beings. To me there is none hateful or dear. But those who worship me with devotion are in me and I am in them.*

Many followers of Sai Baba visit Shirdi to pray the saint will grant them the gift of a child. After my father's death, I was determined to seek Baba's help for myself by going there. I did not know that when I finally went to Shirdi, Sai Baba would guide me in a different direction — towards helping others through the gift of healing.

6
DISCOVERING THE
GIFT OF HEALING

My first opportunity to do regular healing came about by chance, soon after my father's death. I was suffering from very bad backaches and faced the possibility of another operation for a retrovert uterus. A friend told me about a clinic near where we lived where they cured by the laying on of hands. There were no doctors on the staff. The man in charge — a businessman from Bangalore — had learned how to do this laying on of hands in London from the famous English healer, Harry Edwards. I was fed up with regular doctors and decided to see if they could help me at the clinic.

I was particularly interested in the idea that one could touch someone and heal them. Ever since my father's death, whenever anyone was sick, I had wanted to go and touch that person. Somehow I believed that if I could just touch that person, he or she would be healed. Whenever I heard someone in the neighborhood was ill, I wanted to go to them. The urge was so strong, I myself felt uncomfortable, but I only felt this need when I heard anyone was ill, otherwise I never thought about it.

When I went to the clinic they questioned me about my problem, then told me to lie down. The man in charge and two or three of the ladies who were his helpers put their hands on my back. "How do you feel?" they asked after ten to fifteen minutes.

"I don't feel anything," I said. I was very disappointed. "You must come for treatment until you are cured," they instructed me.

I kept coming for treatment and although I didn't feel better, they insisted I must be. Later I realized this method was really a form of positive thinking, not the laying on of hands I had expected. Patients were told over and over that they were becoming better and better. When I told them at the clinic that I would soon have to have an operation, I was advised to write to Mr. Edwards in London and ask for absent healing. I postponed my operation while I waited to see if the absent healing would help.

Even though I had not got results myself, I asked the ladies if I could join them in trying to heal others. They agreed to let me. By this time the clinic was managed by a wonderful woman and a very genuine healer, a Mrs. Narang, known to everyone as "Bado." From the very beginning she was fond of me and although she was unable to help my own physical problems, her encouragement of my healing played an important role in what I am today.

One day I noticed my right hand started to vibrate when I put it on a sick person, and that the vibration was greatest at the place of the actual trouble where the patient felt pain. On its own the vibration would stop and the patient would start to feel better.

I became a little frightened about the vibration in my hand. I started praying I did not have the dreaded Parkinson's disease. When I confessed my fears to my husband, he was even more against my working at the clinic. "You are very sick already, you are making yourself more ill, you should stop working there," he reproached me. "It's all right for these society ladies but you have more than enough to do at home."

In spite of his anxiety, I felt I had to continue at the clinic because it seemed that just by putting my right hand on people I could diagnose their problems. I was also glad to be treating mostly poorer people who did not have money for medical doctors. As time went on I found I was working not only on spinal problems but on more difficult and unusual cases.

Unfortunately my success led to trouble with some of the other ladies at the clinic. "You spend too much time with patients," they complained. "Why do you shake your hand in that funny way? Why don't you follow our methods?"

"As long as my hand vibrates on a patient, I must continue to treat that patient," I told them, "that is my way of healing."

"Shaking your hand can't possibly make any difference" they insisted, but I refused to give in. As I got more experience I became increasingly convinced that my right hand had some kind of healing power and I followed my own intuition. I also noticed that in spite of their protests the ladies had all started bringing their friends and relatives to me for treatment.

In the meantime my own condition was becoming more and more serious. Mr. Edwards' absent healing had not helped me and I decided I must have the operation. I was determined to go to the best gynecologist in India — the internationally famous Dr. Shirodkar in Bombay. I also had another reason for choosing this doctor: I knew that Shirdi, where Sai Baba had lived, was not far from Bombay. My husband promised that after the operation he would take me to the temple in Shirdi dedicated to Baba.

Immediately after the operation I was in acute pain. My body was bandaged and I couldn't make out where the pain was coming from. The clinic doctors sent my husband to the chemist to buy a particular painkiller. While he was out, the pain increased until it became unbearable. When I felt most desperate I suddenly remembered the healing power of my right hand. I put that hand to the side where the doctor had told me he was going to make the incision, but my hand kept pulling to the center. After only a few minutes, the pain was gone.

When my husband came back I told him how my hand had vibrated and stopped the pain. Later when the doctor took off the bandage, I saw he had changed his mind and made the incision in the center. I was very much surprised and, for the first time, I truly believed in my healing gift.

After a few days I asked my husband when we would go to Shirdi. "I'm afraid Shirdi's too far from Bombay for you to go in your condition," he said. I started crying. "You know how weak you are and in so much pain," he said, "if you went on a journey like that now you would only get ill again." I continued to weep and he finally went back to our hotel.

It was a Thursday evening, I now know Thursdays are special to Sai Baba. When I was alone in the room, one of the nurses came in. I was too upset to pay attention to what she was saying. In my mind I was reproaching Sai Baba: "You know the operation wasn't the real reason I came to Bombay. You know I planned to visit Shirdi. Why are you treating me like this?" Suddenly I heard the nurse say the words, "Sai Baba."

"What did you say?" I asked her.

"There is a Sai Baba temple near the nursing home," she explained. "If you are not well enough to visit Shirdi, I'll be happy to take you to the temple when you leave here."

The day I was to leave the nursing home I was so sick I could hardly stand, but they would not allow me to stay any longer. Though my husband was very angry with me, I went with the nurse to the Sai Baba temple on our way to the hotel. The temple was in a private home, and they had a life-sized marble statue of Sai Baba in his characteristic sitting position. His statue was colored so cleverly it looked like a real person, it was as if the saint was there in flesh and blood. I felt my ambition to see Baba had been fulfilled. It is impossible to describe what peace and comfort I received from that visit.

At the hotel, I continued to be in a lot of pain. In the mornings I would get up and walk about slowly as instructed by the doctor, but with great difficulty. Then, one night I saw Sai Baba. He was standing near my bed, bending over me. He told me, "My child, today all your pain will vanish and you will feel all right." All my life I have had very vivid dreams and, still to this day, I cannot be sure whether seeing Baba that night was a dream or an actual vision.

The next morning I still had a lot of pain and I thought it must all have been a dream. As I started walking slowly round the bed, my husband, seeing me in such pain, said he would beg the doctor to take me back in the nursing home. "Today I will be all right," I replied calmly.

When I went to take my bath, it was as if I threw away my pain as I removed my clothes. I could stand up straight! It was then I told my husband about the vision of Sai Baba. He could not believe his eyes, seeing me erect and without pain. Since that time, I have had many visions of Sai Baba.

Before we returned to New Delhi I asked my husband to visit the Sai Baba temple in Bombay. He returned with flowers and *prasad* blessed at the temple and we had a safe, uneventful journey home.

Some time later we were able to return to Bombay and my husband took me to Shirdi. It was a wonderful visit. We arrived in what was then the quiet little town of Shirdi shortly before the noon *puja* (prayers) started. When I ran into the temple, everyone was standing in pindrop silence waiting for the exact moment when the *arte* (ovation) would begin. Just as I reached Sai Baba's statue, all the bells rang and the musicians started to play. It was as if they had been waiting only for me. As I stood there with the incense thick around me, uplifted by the sacred music and the nearness of Baba, I felt a sudden longing for a tiny rosebud lying near the feet of the saint's statue. Should I ask the priest to give it me? No, I didn't like to ask for a special favor when there were so many others there. He must somehow have understood my need. Without saying anything the priest walked forward, picked up the rosebud and gave it to me. Even after so many years, I still have the faded petals.

As I sat on the floor of the temple to pray, I asked Baba for the gift of a child. Then almost without conscious thought I found myself saying, "Baba, show me the path I must follow."

7
TURNING POINTS

After we'd returned to New Delhi, as soon as I felt strong enough, I again began working at the clinic. I was not getting much support from the other ladies and my husband was more and more against my being there. Having visited Shirdi and prayed for a child, I kept hoping I would conceive. I would have given up the healing in my longing to have children if I had not felt an inner force compelling me to continue.

I was also troubled during this period by a strange, recurring dream. In this dream my body becomes more and more huge and heavy, I feel I am a tiny ant being crushed by the weight of an elephant. When I wake up, I wonder if it is my body or my soul that is being crushed. Even more disturbing, I suffered the same feelings of suffocation one afternoon when resting but wide awake. I cannot move, I am being crushed by the weight of my body. After a few minutes the sensation passed, but I was left exhausted and with a terrible headache. Years later, at a lecture on awakening the *kundalini shakti* (serpent or creative power), I learned that this feeling of the body's unbearable heaviness is frequently experienced by those whose *kundalini shakti* is being aroused.

I also suffered at this time from disorientation. One night in particular, I woke at midnight from a heavy sleep. I had no idea where I was. I did not recognize my husband beside me and I felt very frightened. Slowly by the glow of the night light, I made out familiar pictures and furniture. I knew who my husband was. All the rest of the night and the whole next day I had a splitting headache and was haunted by a feeling of loss. I knew I could not remember something very important. Perhaps it was the glimpse of a past life?

In this anxious, disturbed state I was sorting through my books late one night, when a volume of Tagore's poems fell from the shelf. It opened at these lines:

To whomsoever you hand over your flag, give the person courage, love and devotion so that he may carry it to the end of his life.

I was convinced the words had a special meaning for me, that they were a message from Sai Baba. I must carry his "flag"— this gift of healing —however painful and heavy the burden might be. I must not leave this noble work. God had filled my heart with so much devotion and love I must carry it till the end of my life.

Some time after this incident, I was taken to Shirdi for a second visit by a great devotee of the saint, a patient I had cured of a spinal problem. I prayed to Baba, "You have shown me my path. I don't want anything for myself anymore, but I have a friend who is like a sister, she has lost her son, will you grant her the gift of a child?"

Soon after I returned to Delhi from Shirdi, my friend told me she had conceived. "My prayer has been answered," I told her. She and her husband became lifelong followers of Sai Baba and their child has been like a son to me.

A Second Turning Point

Another turning point in my life came during the visit to the clinic of a Lebanese woman and her husband. I was asked to examine the woman's eyes. As I put my hand near her head, my hand told me one eye was much worse than the other. As my hand vibrated near that eye, her husband suddenly looked up from his book. "Why are you shaking your hand like that?" he asked.

"What you call 'shaking' is an automatic motion of my hand," I said. "I am concentrating on the right eye because my hand tells me that is where the problem is. When the vibration stops, I will know the treatment is over for the day."

"Isn't that amazing," his wife said to him. "I never told her my right eye was my bad eye."

"She's seen from your glasses that your right eye is weak," he said. He spoke in Arabic, but it was not hard to understand his meaning. Then he made me more angry by asking again why I shook my hand.

When I'd finished the treatment, I touched the wife lightly on the back to tell her the treatment was over. Immediately my hand started to vibrate. "Do you have any problems with your spine?" I asked. She said she had.

"You see," she turned to her husband, "she *can* diagnose with her hand. You know I didn't tell her anything about my back."

At this point her husband suddenly became very curious. "Can you find out what my problem is?" he asked.

"I can tell you in just one minute if you let me examine you," I flashed back. I should not have boasted, but he'd upset me with his scoffing questions and in those days I was so excited, so puffed up with pride about my powers. Then I said, "I don't have too much more time at the clinic today, so just tell me whether your problem is in the front or the back of your body."

"In the front, but I want you to examine me away from all these other people," he said.

I took him out onto the terrace and asked him to lie down on a bench there. I began to check him in my usual way by moving my right hand down the body, holding it about six inches away, starting from the head. This is how I always do the diagnosis. It seems that some sort of electrical field is built up and my hand vibrates most strongly at the actual site of the problem. As my hand came near his lower abdomen, it started to vibrate very hard.

"Your problem is there," I pointed to his lower abdomen. He didn't say anything then, but he told me later he was amazed that I had been able to immediately locate the colitis he'd been suffering from for the previous three months.

I vibrated my hand over that area for ten to fifteen minutes. When my hand stopped moving I told him the treatment was over. I was still upset with him and did not ask how he felt. When I knew him better he told me he had been astonished how much better he felt from my touch.

The next time he came to the clinic with his wife he was completely different. He wanted to know all about me, what sort of cases I could handle, what my rate of success was. Then he told me why he was so interested. "Will you go with me to the Syrian Embassy to treat my friend the ambassador?" he asked. "He has a very badly slipped disc and is in constant pain. He's not able to lift his right hand or even to write."

"I've helped lots of slipped disc cases," I told him, "but I must ask my husband's permission to visit your friend."

After they had left I discovered that the gentleman was Dr. Ala-ud-Din Drooby, a famous neuro-psychiatrist on leave from the American Hospital in Beirut. I felt quite miserable. If I'd known he was a doctor, I'd never have boasted to him in this manner.

The Syrian ambassador was a charming, cultured man, a famous Arab poet, who had been in India for fifteen to twenty years. He told me straight away, "I don't believe in faith healing. I'm scheduled to go abroad for surgery in a few days. The only reason I'm seeing you is because Dr. Drooby brought you here. If you still want to treat me, knowing all this, you are most welcome."

"Your faith in me plays no part in my healing, " I explained to him. "I don't myself know how I heal. I will only touch you. If it works, well and good. If not, you forget about me and I'll forget all about you. You don't have to condition your mind to anything."

I told him to relax and I put my hand on his spine. When the vibration stopped after about twenty minutes I didn't ask how he felt.

"Oh, my God," he exclaimed, "I can lift my arm! There is no pain!" He grabbed his coat and put it on. He lifted a chair. He was so excited, he kept saying over and over, "I can't believe it, I can't believe it!" Then he rushed to the phone and invited several friends to come over immediately to meet "the miraculous lady who's healed me."

Dr. Drooby, too, was very happy. "Didn't I tell you she has a healing power in her right hand?" he said. I was truly surprised myself, but I told the ambassador I knew from experience he could not be cured in one sitting, I would have to treat him several times.

My whole life changed as a result of this healing. The ambassador and his wife wanted me to help a lot of their friends, and asked if I would open a clinic in their home which was also the embassy. After discussing it with my husband and obtaining his consent, it was arranged I should treat people at the embassy three times a week.

Initially, I carried on with my work at the clinic near me. However some of the ladies told me I was creating disharmony because all the patients wanted to be treated only by me. Also they told me I must start asking for donations. I didn't feel I could do this. I have never thought I should charge for my healing. I believe it is a gift from God and nothing for which I should seek a material reward.

My husband had retired only a few weeks before. I talked it over with him, and we decided I should treat patients six days a week, three days at the Syrian Embassy and three days at our own home. A few months after I left the other clinic it was closed and Mrs. Narang opened a clinic in another part of Delhi. In spite of my problems there, "Bado" and I remained good friends until her death some years later.

8
SOME EARLY CASES

With my clinics at home and at the Syrian Embassy, I was working very hard. Suddenly a lot of people had heard about me and came for treatment. For the first time in my life I felt truly appreciated and wanted, that I was more than just a wife, that I was someone in my own right.

Initially I had treated mostly spinal cases because I had the idea they were the only ones I could heal. Now I began to take on other kinds of problems. With every new case I was discovering what my gift was able to achieve. The few doctors who believed in my healing tended to send me cases for which they had no cures, and it was a great help to have the advice of Dr. Drooby who was still in New Delhi.

One of the first patients I treated at home was a young boy with double vision. I was hesitant to take the case as the doctors suspected a brain tumor, but my husband and Dr. Drooby both urged me to take up the challenge. When I put my hand near the boy's head, it was drawn not to the skull but to his eyes.

"Tell me about your general health," I asked the boy because somehow I felt sure it couldn't be a brain tumor. After some probing, I learned he suffered from very bad chronic sinusitis. The reason my hand had gone to his eyes was because a hard lump had formed in the sinuses and blocked circulation to the optic nerves. By vibrating my hand over the area I was able to dissolve the lump and restore his eyesight to normal in only a few sittings. Since then I have treated many patients suffering double vision from different causes.

Another of my first child patients was sent to me by a neighbor. The boy's eyeball had been removed from its socket for cancer and the wound would not heal. The doctor had told the family that cancer would probably recur within five years and that the child's eyebrows would never grow back. After two to three treatments of the bandaged eye, the wound started to heal and the boy's eyebrows started to grow. This was the first time I discovered that my gift would heal wounds.

When the doctor removed the bandage, the boy's mother told me he had been delighted. "The wound is healed," he'd exclaimed, "no need for any more treatment." The mother told me she could now take the boy home to Dehra Dun.

"I don't like to go against a doctor's opinion, but my hand is still vibrating over your son's eye. I must not end the treatment until my hand stops," I said. When his mother next brought the boy to my home clinic, together we examined the eye socket with a magnifying glass and saw that a tiny pinpoint was still raw. "I am sure that is the reason my hand still vibrates," I told her and I continued to treat the child until my hand stopped moving.

Many years later, at a wedding party in Delhi, a woman approached me. "Do you remember me?" she asked. I have seen so many patients over the years, and so much time had passed, that I was not really sure who she was. Then she pointed to a tall young man of eighteen in the crowd wearing dark glasses. "That is the boy you saved."

I would like to have spoken to him, but I thought to myself, when they needed me I helped them, but why should I now tell that boy "I have healed you." It is God who healed him, I was only the instrument.

Another early patient was the Indian Chief of Protocol. He had been to his family doctor because he was feeling a tightness in his chest. "Now he's told me I have a serious heart problem, but I'd like your opinion because he's not really a heart specialist," he confided to me. "Will you check me and tell me what you think." When I held my hand over his body, I found nothing wrong with his heart. However, I could diagnose with my hand that he was suffering from spondylitis (inflammation of the vertebrae), his neck was very stiff and his blood was not flowing properly between his head and his heart, especially in certain positions.

"Please go and see the best heart specialist in Bombay," I told him. "See if he confirms my diagnosis that it is the pressure on the back of your spine, not your heart, that is causing your symptoms." From the Bombay specialist's X-rays, it could be seen the problem was in his spine. He returned to Delhi, very happy, and I was able to cure the spondylitis and other problems with only a few treatments.

One day a young niece of my husband's became ill. She had a very high fever and the family asked me to go and examine her while they were waiting for the doctor to come. My husband came with me as he, too, was concerned about the child. When our family doctor arrived he diagnosed flu as both parents had just recovered from it.

"Please excuse me, doctor," I said, "but there is something wrong with the child's throat." I showed him how my hand vibrated there. He looked surprised, but said nothing to me.

My husband was still a little embarrassed about my healing power and said to our doctor, laughing, "My wife thinks she has become a doctor, she helps so many people." Our doctor knew us both very well and asked for an explanation about what I thought I was doing.

"I feel I have some healing power in my right hand," I told him. "Please, first you attend the child, then I will tell you everything."

When he'd looked at the child's throat, the doctor told us she had a septic tonsil. Then he turned to my husband. "My God, she is gifted," he said. "She is your wife — don't make fun of her. One person in a million is born with this sort of power."

When he was leaving he asked if I would treat his wife for a persistent back pain. She came to see me a few days later and while I was treating her she told me what her husband had said about me. "With this sort of gift, her husband will not be able to hide her. The world will take her away. She is a very simple person, she has no idea of what she has got in her hand, but God has given her the gift."

Another case I treated at this time was that of a Nepalese girl, about three years old, who had been born with a hole in her heart. Her mother was very distressed as the child had almost no energy and the doctors were advising a major operation. It was very difficult to treat her as she refused to lie down on my treatment bed and I had to work while she relaxed in her mother's arms. After a few visits the mother told me she did not need to come anymore as the child could play like other children without tiring. When they returned to Nepal the doctors said surgery was no longer needed.

Another child patient was born a "blue" baby and put on oxygen in intensive care immediately after delivery. The mother was fretting for her child and the young doctor in charge was worried about her health. He knew me and asked if I would come to the hospital to help. After only five treatments, the tiny baby's color was normal and she was able to be with her mother.

The surgeon who'd delivered the baby was amazed and asked what had happened. He was very interested to hear about my healing and some time later asked me to help his brother-in-law, a major-general in the army. "The army doctors say my brother-in-law has a heart murmur," he told me. "He's due for promotion, but if he fails the next test, he's been told he'll be retired. You can imagine how worried he is. Will you see if you can help him?"

"I've only treated a three-year-old child for heart trouble, I have no idea if I can help," I said.

"Just please see him," he urged, "but can you tell me how much you are charging?" He was very surprised to hear I would not accept any payment. I gave the major-general several treatments and he was able to pass the sophisticated heart test given to pilots without any problem. He was promoted to lieutenant-general and served his full term.

As always, one patient passes on another patient to me. Some time later, this lieutenant-general asked me to treat one of his officers for two blockages in the artery. This was my first case of this type and I was very interested to know if my gift would be able to help.

This problem required a long course of treatments. I gave the officer three sittings a week for many weeks until my hand stopped vibrating. Some years later the same officer telephoned. He told me he was now a lieutenant-colonel and wanted to bring his wife and daughter to meet me. I could hardly recognize him, he was a different person. He told me that just before his promotion was due, he had had to have an angiogram and he had been promoted when the doctors found his heart was perfectly normal.

One day the Syrian ambassador introduced me to James George, the Canadian High Commissioner to India, a spiritual man and very well read. The ambassador wanted me to help Mr. George who had developed a sizeable soft lump on his right shoulder blade that was slowly increasing in size. "The doctors are saying he should have surgery immediately," the ambassador told me, "but it sounds very dangerous because of the position of the tumor and the very long operation involved."

"Have you had a biopsy? Do you have any pain?" I asked Mr. George. He told me he'd had no biopsy or pain but that he couldn't sleep on his back and had trouble lifting his right arm.

I treated James George for one month, every day except Sundays. At first, my hand used to vibrate for about one hour. As my hand vibrated less and less, the soft lump slowly hardened and became smaller and looser from the body. After one month exactly, the vibrations stopped.

He went for surgery and the operation took just twenty minutes. The doctors found only dead tissue, there was not even any loss of blood when they operated. The lump was not malignant. As he explained in his Foreword to this book, James George is convinced my healing changed the lump into a non-malignant growth as well as reducing its size and shape so the operation could be performed without danger. I also treated his wife for spondylitis and, still to the day, we are all good friends.

"There Is Someone Standing Behind You"

About this time I had a very strange experience, my first encounter with a clairvoyant. The Syrian ambassador asked me to treat a couple who had come to Delhi from Paris for a short visit. The wife had had food poisoning and I was able to relieve her gastric problem with one sitting. Then the husband asked me to treat him for a back problem. Before I started to work on him, he studied my face for several minutes very carefully. "She has psychic eyes," he told the ambassador.

I asked the man to lie down and, as is my custom, I closed the door in the dimly lighted room. When I put my hand on his back, he suddenly asked me, "Who is standing behind you?" I looked behind me. "There is no one there."

"Of course there is, there is a man standing behind you," he insisted.

Again I looked over my shoulder. I felt a little frightened. I repeated, "No, there is no one there." Then I added, "There was a very famous saint, people say He is the one who helps me in my healing." As I said this, I heard a man laugh very loudly. I could feel from holding my hand on my patient's back, it was not he who had laughed. I got frightened and took my hand away.

My patient said, "You are right, I did not laugh. It was the saint. You finish treating me and I will tell you everything. Now I understand the message I received."

When I had finished my treatment, he gave me an exact description of the man he'd seen standing behind me — how he was tall and thin with high cheekbones and blue eyes, how he wore a headband. It was a perfect description of Sai Baba. "Do you have a picture of the saint?" he asked me. I showed him the Sai Baba medallion I always wear on a chain around my neck. "Yes," he said, "that is the man and this is the message he gave me.

"When you said he was a great saint, he laughed. He loves you like a daughter. He is very fond of you, but he says you must not work so hard. There will be an ocean of sick people, you cannot cure them all. You must select your cases, you must not work every day, otherwise you will not live very long. You must take care of yourself."

I was stunned to hear all this. The man left the room and, as usual, there were many people waiting to see me. He told them about the whole incident, and he specifically told them I must not be worked too hard.

The famous German architect, Karl Heinz, and his wife Bella were in the crowd waiting for me. Both of them were my patients, I used to treat Karl for emphysema. Bella came to our home and told my husband the whole story, and how this patient was known to have special clairvoyant powers that must have enabled him to see Sai Baba.

After this, I regulated my work. My husband had scolded me many times for working six days a week and seeing too many patients — for what he called "burning the candle at both ends." I cut my time down to three to four days a week and I started choosing cases. Still to this day I am following Sai Baba's instructions.

Over the years, I have learned which cases I can treat most successfully. I find I am not successful with arthritis or rheumatism, or with any kind of skin problem. I am not able to cure chronic diseases like multiple sclerosis and Parkinson's. I have treated some cancer cases, but I prefer not to as it drains so much of my energy and I am never sure I have been able to effect a complete cure. Also, my hand does not vibrate over patients who have had massive radiation or chemotherapy. I believe this is because my healing cannot help if the immune system is too damaged. I have thought about it a great deal and I have decided that if I am able to help some people more than others, I should save my gift for those I can help. But it is always very painful to have to turn anyone away.

9

VISIT TO BEIRUT

Dr. Drooby was due to return to Beirut, and he asked me to come to Lebanon to visit the American Hospital where he worked. My husband was not very keen on my going, but the Syrian ambassador, Omar Abu Riche, had arranged for my ticket and he and his wife Munira would put me up in their Beirut home. Eventually my husband agreed, grudgingly, I should go. I did not want to leave unless I had his full approval.

Some days before I was due to go, my husband went for his morning walk with our dog and slipped and hurt his knee badly. He did not tell me he'd hurt himself and when I came back from my clinic at the Syrian Embassy, I found him in great pain. His sister, who was very fond of him, was sitting with him and she was furious with me. "Here your husband is sick and you are out helping other people, busy with your social work. He's had an accident and you are not in the least bothered — you are planning to go out of India and leave him with a fractured leg!"

"He said nothing to me about his fall," I told her, and without saying anything else to her, I began to treat my husband's knee. It was cold and he was in great pain. I covered him with a blanket and, over his protests, I went on working on his knee through the blanket until midnight when he told me he was feeling much better. Only when I was sure he could get up and walk without using a stick did I go to bed.

The next day he was still much better and in a happy mood. He told me I should go to the passport office to collect my passport. After that he went out and made all the other arrangements for my travel — visas, foreign exchange, and so on. I could see a big change in him. It seemed as if it were God's hand. If he had not fallen and hurt himself, and if I had not had the chance to heal him myself, he would not have been so willing to have me go.

I left for Beirut at night, my first trip outside India and traveling alone. Suddenly I remembered Tagore's lines:

Oh, my lonely traveler, you have to start your journey at night.
Beware, you have to cross insurmountable mountains, vast oceans,
and the barren deserts.

I thought this might have been written for me. I was sure I would have to face crowds of hostile doctors and that had always made me feel very nervous. Doctors study for so many long, hard years. How could I, with no medical qualifications, put myself up as equal to them? Omar Abu Riche had so many times wanted me to meet doctors when I was working in the clinic at the Syrian Embassy, but I had always refused. I felt I was only an ordinary person and that I should remain humble as it was only in this way that I would be able to serve humanity and give meaning to the words "spiritual healing." My only support then in my lone journey was my strong faith in God. I knew His blessings were with me. With all humility I started my journey to this country new and strange to me.

In those days Beirut was not a sad and war-torn city. Small and beautiful, it was called "The Paris of the Middle East" for its elegant hotels, shops and restaurants and its cosmopolitan, French-speaking people. If you wanted to, you could spend the morning on the beach and in the afternoon drive up excellent roads to ski in the beautiful, snow-capped mountains. The quality of medical care was internationally famous and people all over the region came to the American Hospital where Dr. Drooby was the head neuro-psychiatrist.

My first day in Beirut a Syrian lady, Mrs. Jallad, came to meet me. Dr. Drooby had previously recommended she go to India to see me for a medical problem the doctors could not solve. The night before I arrived, she dreamed she felt my vibrations on her troubled body. When Dr. Drooby telephoned to tell her I was in Beirut, she exclaimed, "I knew it," and told him of her dream. When we met she said, "I have already had your first treatment."

The American Hospital in Beirut

My first encounter in Beirut was a pleasant one but the next day, when Dr. Drooby took me to the hospital to meet the doctors there, I could sense they were very skeptical. However they immediately wanted me to work on a serious case of brain injury. The patient was an architect and engineer and also a commando leader. While supervising a construction job, someone had deliberately dropped a sack of heavy stones on his head, crushing it, and a portion of his brain had come out. By the time I arrived at the hospital the patient had already had brain surgery, but pneumonia had developed and he was lying on a block of ice to bring down the fever. He was on an artificial respirator with a tube inserted into the affected lung.

They wanted me to work on his head injury, but I did not dare put my hand on his head in case my vibrations disturbed the surgery. Then they asked me to work on the right lung to loosen the congestion so they could clear his lung by suction. I found my hand vibrated over the left lung, not the right. They went to check the X-rays and discovered to their horror they had put the tube in the wrong lung.

After this, the doctors' attitude towards me changed greatly. I went on working on the affected lung until the congestion became less and less and the patient's temperature started to come down. Each time I came to the hospital after this, they asked me to check his vital organs. One time, for example, my hand vibrated over his kidneys and they found he had a urinary infection.

All the doctors except the neurosurgeon acknowledged my hand always diagnosed correctly. While I was working on the patient's lungs one day, my hand was pulled towards his head. I suspected something must be wrong with the way the wound was healing and asked the doctors present to please ask the surgeon to change the bandage and inspect the head wound. One of the doctors was the patient's brother who had come from the United States to help. He, too, urged the surgeon to look at the wound. "All is well," the surgeon insisted, "I will continue to change the bandage every third day." Sadly, when the surgeon finally did change the bandage, he discovered that the patient's head wound was severely infected and the unfortunate man died on the spot.

Slowly the number of patients coming to me increased. In the morning I worked at the hospital, in the evening at the Syrian ambassador's home. Most of the cases were spinal problems, similar to the one I had treated for the ambassador — slipped discs and spondylitis. I remember I cured one young boy's slipped disc at one sitting. I could hardly believe it myself. His family owned a bakery shop and he came back next day with a big cake for me with my name written on it in bold, chocolate-icing letters.

One day I was interviewed by the local newspaper. They wrote about my work and featured a big picture of me showing how my hand vibrates. It became very difficult to handle the crowd attracted by the article and I began to get very tired. So many people wanted to be treated by me it was quite frightening.

The Blessed Sharbel

To give me a little break, my friends took me to the mountains to visit the tomb of Sharbel, the hermit of Lebanon. The blessed Sharbel had led a solitary life of penance and mortification high up in the mountains where he used to pray and meditate, surviving on bread and water given weekly by the villagers.

I visited this barren place and saw the crude stone shelter where Sharbel slept on the bare floor with a rock for his pillow. It is said that when he died in 1905, an extraordinary brightness surrounded his first tomb. It was opened four months after his death to take the body to a larger mausoleum, and the saint's body was found to be incorrupt — as if it had been buried the same day. A blood-like liquid was dripping from the body. I was told this liquid is still collected devoutly in bottles and is said to give relief and to sometimes cure the sick.

Many miracles have been attributed to the saint. I felt the great sense of piety that surrounds the tomb and attracts thousands of pilgrims each year from all over the world. I also saw thousands of letters, kept in a special archive, and the many crutches, walking sticks, and glasses left behind by those who are cured. I reflected how Sharbel, living a solitary life dedicated to the love of God, induces us in the midst of this restless and materialistic world to be silent in order to meet God and to establish an interior peace in our soul. There we can listen to the appeals of grace, the grace necessary for salvation.

I Encounter Another Clairvoyant

I was taken by my friend Munira, the Syrian ambassador's wife, to meet the Minister of the Interior, Kamal beg Zumlat. He was a member of the Druse, an Islamic sect headquartered in southern Lebanon. Although he held a very important and powerful position, he was a highly spiritual man whose guru was in south India. I thought he must want to meet me because I was also from India.

When we arrived at the office in his home, there was a long line of people waiting to meet him. When I was called to see him he became absorbed in a long discussion of my work and of his spiritual life. I began to feel uneasy, thinking of the long line outside. "Thank you for seeing me, but I think I should leave now. You have so many people waiting to see you," I said.

"No, no, you must stay for dinner," he insisted. As I went with Munira and two other ladies through his palatial home, we passed through his bedroom. I was impressed to see he slept on a simple bed on the floor with only a rough blanket for cover. I learned later his wife had left him because he insisted on such a Spartan life.

When we sat down to dinner with Mr. Zumlat, I noticed an odd looking person sitting in one corner of the room. He did not join us for our simple vegetarian dinner and he was not introduced to me. While we were eating the man spoke in Arabic to the ladies with me. "Can you show us how you do your treatment?" Munira then asked me. As Munira wears glasses, it seemed simplest to demonstrate on her eyes. As my hand vibrated I noticed the man watching me intently. Then he said something in Arabic that made them all very excited.

On the way home, Munira told me Mr. Zumlat wanted to know about my gift. He had called in this queer looking man, who had special powers, to find out what kind of power I had. "He told us, 'When she starts working, lightning passes through her from head to foot, and there is a figure of a man standing behind her. When her hand stops vibrating, the figure also disappears.'"

When Mr. Zumlat came to dinner with us, he told me this man had taught him to meditate. While they meditated, this man's spiritual guide — invisible to Mr. Zumlat — would also come. "How do I know the guide is with us?" he'd asked his mentor. "My guide is standing near the door," his mentor told him. "You try to pass through the door and you will find you cannot pass." Mr. Zumlat said that when he'd tried to go out through that door, he'd bumped into a figure he could not see. He was convinced that this spirit was the one who guided him in his day-to-day work.

During our last meeting in Beirut, Mr. Zumlat gave me some advice. "You will not be able to pass on your healing gift," he told me, "but you must write about whatever knowledge you have of herbs and natural cures so that others can benefit from them." I learned some years later that Mr. Zumlat had been shot dead by an unknown man. I was shocked and saddened that such a spiritual man, of such high intellect and learning, had died that way. However I have been told that whenever a person gets involved with a spirit, they are likely to risk some form of violent death.

As my stay in Beirut drew to a close I was very tired and not feeling well. The wife of the leading dress designer persuaded me to visit her husband. He was lying in a huge bed surrounded by lacy pillows. He had had a serious, paralyzing stroke on the left side of his body, and when I put my hand on his body it did not vibrate as the brain cells were too damaged. He told his wife in a halting voice that he had seen me treating him in a dream and he had felt so much better. When he saw me in person he said, "In my dream she was laughing all the time, now she is not even smiling." It is true that when I treat people I always smile and laugh, but that day I was feeling too tired and unwell. So my trip began with a dream and ended with a dream also.

Doctors Test Me for ESP

Just two days before I went home I was approached by a group of some twenty doctors and scientists visiting Beirut from England and the United States. They had seen the newspaper article about me and were anxious to meet me as they were investigating instances of extra sensory perception (ESP). I had no idea they really only wanted to challenge me when I agreed to meet them; I was interested in learning from them more about my own gift. As I've said, at home in India I had always been too nervous to meet a group of doctors like this, but after working in the American Hospital with so many famous doctors, I had no fear of this group.

When we first met they surrounded and observed me as if I were an inanimate object. Then they all started asking me questions at once. I told them straight out: "Don't ask me any medical questions — I don't have any medical knowledge at all. I have no idea about my gift; I can only show you my work. Then you can ask me any questions you like after that. If you like I can also tell you about any problems you may have with your own health."

I don't remember all the questions they asked me, but I do remember they asked if I was interested in making money by healing people. "I never take money from people," I said, "my healing power is a gift from God."

"Are you interested in good food or in other physical comforts?" was another question. "I am not the least interested in things like that," I told them. "What I like to do is to meditate and sometimes I want to be all alone. I love the sea and rivers, or any contact with nature, like a garden. I long to be in close contact with nature. Mountains also give me the sense of God's nearness. In silence I feel I am nearer to him, perhaps I am wrong? Whenever I have questions I need to answer, I go out onto our terrace and slowly I feel the answer in my brain, very clearly. I feel happy in helping other people." They told me that people with true ESP always answered the same way.

However, unknown to me, they still wanted to test me. One of the doctors told me he was perfectly healthy, but would I examine him anyway. "Please lie down," I told him and I started my diagnosis by moving my right hand down his body. As I brought my hand over his heart, it started vibrating. That put me in a quandary. Here was a doctor who'd told me he was perfectly well, but my hand told me otherwise. I decided I had to tell him what I thought. "You may be a doctor," I said, "but you apparently don't know there may be something wrong with your heart. I think you have a problem there and you should get yourself checked with an ECG (electro-cardiogram) as soon as possible. There would be no harm in getting that done." I didn't know that the doctor himself and all the other doctors and scientists there knew the man had a bad heart. I could see, however, they all looked very surprised.

"Frankly I had a heart attack two years ago," the doctor told me. "Now I have a pain in my back. Will you check it for me, please?" I checked it and gave him a few minutes treatment, and he told me he felt much better. Then several of the other doctors and scientists asked me to check them.

That day God was with me. All the cases I diagnosed proved to be correct and they all praised me for the speed and accuracy with which I diagnosed their problems. Only at the end did they tell me they had asked to meet me so they could challenge me.

They also asked me to take part in another experiment. Whenever I go to a mosque, church, or temple — any holy place of worship — invariably my whole body starts vibrating, especially my right hand. They wanted me to hold some film to see what would happen. Unfortunately, the day we were to go to the mosque it was raining so heavily the plan had to be abandoned.

The day after I'd met the group, one of the doctors wrote an article for the local press, with my picture. I have not kept the clipping, but can still remember part of what was written: "The lady has got something, we cannot define it, but there is no doubt she can diagnose the part of the body which has some problem, and there is no doubt about the wonderful healing energy she possesses." The Syrian ambassador brought this article to my husband and told him he hoped he would have no more doubts about my healing power. In fact, the greatest gain from the journey was the change in my husband. He finally accepted I did truly have the gift of healing.

"You Belong to All Religions"

Shortly after I returned to India, Omar Abu Riche retired and he and Munira went back to their country. It was a great loss to me to part from two such good friends. I remember one day at the Syrian Embassy, shortly before they left India, someone asked me about my religion. "I am a Hindu," I said.

Omar Abu Riche got very angry with me. "In future, don't say you are a Hindu. You belong to all religions. You are only Sree, not even Mrs. Sree Chakravarti. You have come to care for all the sick people. You don't belong to one person or one religion — as Mother is known as Mother only."

I was told the ambassador also spoke about me at one of his farewell parties: "I wish Sree was a precious stone that I could fix in my headdress and carry on my head all my life." This was the love and respect he gave me, and still today I am warmed when I think of all his and his wife's kindness to me.

When the ambassador and his wife had gone, I was asked by several other diplomats to hold my clinic in their homes. I decided, however, that as my husband was a changed person about my healing, I would now work only out of our own home.

10
CURING ULCERS

When I had the clinic at the Syrian Embassy, I worked mostly on healing problems of the spine, the heart, and the eyes. But when an old friend, Mr. Gilani, asked me to treat his gastric ulcer, I found my healing experience expanding.

At first I was reluctant to treat Mr. Gilani because I had never worked on an ulcer before. I told him I didn't have any idea if I could help him. He insisted, however, saying that he'd been to all the best doctors in Delhi and in London for treatment but nothing had ever been permanent. He suggested that I just try and see if a healing would occur.

After some eight to nine sessions with me and sticking to the diet and natural medicines I recommended, he found he was completely cured. His ulcer has never recurred. Since this first case I have worked successfully with many other ulcer patients.

An early ulcer patient was a friend of Mr. Gilani's, Romesh Sethi, who recently retired as General Manager of the Indian Railways. He has written the story of his illness and healing.

Case History: Romesh Sethi

I have always been what is called an A-A personality type — very ambitious, very tense and always striving for excellence. I find it almost impossible to relax mentally and I am constantly putting myself under stress by taking on difficult assignments and challenges. This may be why I got a duodenal ulcer when I was only thirty-two years old. In 1965 my job had taken me to the United Kingdom for six months and the ulcer could also perhaps be traced to a change in diet. In any case, the ulcer started hemorrhaging while I was in England and I had to be hospitalized for four months immediately on my return to Delhi.

For about five years afterwards I suffered from indigestion and a burning sensation in the abdomen after meals, accompanied by gnawing pain. Under a doctor's supervision the ulcers were controlled for four years mainly with a very rigid diet.

The second bleeding attack occurred in May, 1970 when I was passing through a period of severe mental stress. The attack was bad enough to hospitalize me for several months.

After a comparatively healthy period, the third attack happened in October, 1971 without any warning or unusual mental stress. It was only noticed because I felt giddy and had been passing black stools. My hemoglobin count was found to have gone down to 6.5 gm., I began to suffer terrible pain and continued to lose blood.

My doctors decided to operate and a date was set at the All India Institute of Medical Sciences. However, it had to be put off while the doctors continued to build up my hemoglobin count with a course of painful injections to reach a level when it would be safe to operate. It was during this waiting period that my wife and I heard about the miraculous powers of a Mrs. Chakravarti from our friend Mr. Gilani whose ulcer apparently had been cured by her.

When she first examined me, Mrs. Chakravarti surprised me by saying there was no evidence of stomach ulcers when her hand did not vibrate over the suspected area. However, when she made me turn over, her hand started shaking violently on the exact spot where the posterior duodenal ulcer was located. When her fingers occasionally touched the trouble spot, I could feel the vibrations penetrating my body. In the beginning, her hand would vibrate for 25 to 30 minutes each time I went. I used to feel so pain-free and relaxed during her treatment, I would often doze off to sleep! At the end of the treatment, she would wash her hand and then plunge it into clean water and give me this water to take home and drink. (Editor's note: Sree has discontinued this act of transferring her power to water as she has been warned it takes too much of her energy.)

Towards the end of Mrs. Chakravarti's treatments the vibrations became much less and her hand would vibrate for only about five minutes. By this time I could enjoy chatting to her. She was always so bright and friendly and gave sound worldly advice that helped change my attitude to life. One of her great gifts to her patients is to help them change their mental attitudes, to make them feel they can (and must) become physically well, a rare gift indeed.

At the end of the 20 sittings, Mrs. Chakravarti said I should go for another checkup. She was quite confident the ulcers were cured. When I went for an X-ray at the Institute, the technician could only find very faint traces of the large ulcer diagnosed as severe only a few weeks earlier.

Since the traces of the ulcers were barely visible in the new X-rays, the bleeding had stopped and I was no longer suffering from hyper-acidity, the scheduled operation was cancelled. From that time on I have had no recurrence of the ulcers and have even been able to relax my dietary habits — including eating pickles, chilies, and occasionally alcoholic drinks within moderation.

In one's lifetime one finds few if any people like Mrs. Chakravarti. She has never demanded or accepted anything from us or from the many people I had referred to her over the years. Her theory is that if she accepts any reward for her treatment, she will lose the power of healing gifted to her.

I believe the highest state of service to humanity is one in which you help others without expecting any return. Even though Mrs. Chakravarti never asks for anything, there must be a scale somewhere where good deeds keep adding up. She is truly a rare and wonderful person. God bless her!

— Romesh Sethi
New Delhi, India
1992

My only failure with an ulcer patient was an army officer, but I believe it was a matter of his temperament. The officer had severe pain, nausea, and vomiting and the hospital test showed he had an ulcer. He could only come for one treatment a week, but I gave him strict instructions about diet. He improved, but after three sittings he came to me in extreme pain.

"What have you been eating?" I asked. When he told me hard-boiled eggs I told him they are much too hard to digest and probably caused the recurrence.

The next time he came, while he was in my treatment room, he heard a man's voice in the reception room and got very excited. "I know that man," the officer exclaimed, "and under no circumstances are you to treat him. He is a very bad man, a smuggler." At the end of his treatment he burst into the other room and shouted at the man, "You don't deserve to be treated by this spiritual lady." The man got frightened and never came back.

The same officer told me about another incident. He had taken his army troop sightseeing in the Gujrat where they were posted. His men wanted to see a Krishna temple and he asked the guide to tell him its history. When he found the temple had been built to mark the place where Krishna had taken refuge from the battlefield, he got very excited. "It's a disgrace for my men to be in such a temple," he shouted. "Why, if Krishna were alive today, he'd be court-martialed for such action!"

When he told me this story I knew I could never succeed in healing a man with such an excitable temperament. His own nature had caused the ulcer. Soon afterward he got transferred to a distant location and I have not seen him since.

A Diet for Ulcer Patients

Ulcer patients must follow this diet during treatment and continue its use even after they are cured. They will only remain well if they follow the diet very strictly.

In the case of patients with gastric ulcers, I have found that their livers are also always adversely affected, so they must avoid rich, fatty foods that cause liver problems.

For all ulcer patients I recommend the following:

- Eliminate spices and fried foods from your diet.
- Take light meals frequently, preferably of boiled foods, and avoid indigestible foods such as hard-boiled eggs.
- Drink plenty of cold milk.
- An excellent help in the cure is to sip a half cup of cabbage juice during the day.

Another important item in an ulcer-free regime comes from my study of Indian spices and herbs. Particularly important are fenugreek and anise seeds. I also have patients who have been helped by the juice of bael leaves or by a mixture of olive oil and honey.

- Soak overnight in half a glass of water two teaspoons of fenugreek seed and one teaspoon of anise seed. In the morning the water should be drunk on an empty stomach and the seeds discarded. Continue until the ulcer is healed. This is the treatment I recommend most often.
- Some of my patients prefer to take bael-leaf water. Soak seven or eight bael leaves overnight in a glass of water. Strain the water and take first thing in the morning on an empty stomach. Follow this regime for a month. The bael-leaf water forms a coating on the stomach lining that helps heal the ulcer.
- Mix half a teaspoon of pure olive oil with a half teaspoon of honey. Take on an empty stomach first thing in the morning for a month.

These remedies should be tried one at a time, and of the three treatments, I prefer the fenugreek and anise seed mixture.

11
HEALING THROMBO-PHLEBITIS AND HEART AILMENTS

Thrombo-Phlebitis

About the same time I discovered that my hand could help heal ulcers, I confirmed to myself that my gift extended to helping patients with thrombo-phlebitis problems by dissolving blood clots.

One of my early patients, whom I remember very well, was a captain in the army. He had a blood clot in his left hand, near the wrist, which surgeons had tried to remove three times. He had been put on blood thinners, but this too was not successful. He was not allowed out of bed, but having heard about me, he quietly left the hospital and came to my house during evening visiting hours. I had to tell him, "I have no idea if I can help you." He begged me please to try.

I found the clot and my touch was very painful for him. I went on treating him three times a week and the pain became less and less when suddenly he stopped coming. I was very worried until one day he returned, looking terribly pale. "What happened, where have you been?" I asked.

He told me they had given him the wrong injection in hospital. "I was in a coma for two days, and after that I was too weak to leave my bed until tonight." With my treatment he became completely cured and he has sent many cases to me. He always says, "God has made me all right.

Now it is my duty to help others through you." He comes to my house and refuses to leave until I have given him an appointment for his friend.

One day, without any appointment, the captain brought an army officer's wife. The poor woman was in dreadful pain with a very bad case of thrombo-phlebitis. "The doctors want to amputate my arm," she told me, "It's so inflamed and hard to the touch that they are afraid of gangrene."

I found she had one clot in her upper arm and one near her shoulder blade. The moment I touched her arm she screamed, the pain was so bad. "It will be impossible to work if I cannot touch you and use my hand's vibrations to dissolve the clot," I told her.

"Please don't pay any attention to my crying and screaming," she begged me, "Anything is better than losing my arm." During the first treatment her pain improved. After eight sittings both clots dissolved and the color of the arm became normal.

After this case a man came from Lucknow to be treated for some blood clots in his leg. He was in great pain and could not walk properly. The doctors had tried all sorts of treatments and now wanted to amputate. He recovered after eight or nine treatments and has never had a recurrence.

Among my papers I found I had kept a case history prepared by Captain Abdul Kader of the Indian army. It was the Captain's own idea to write up this brief for me in case I should ever have need of it. I believe his case illustrates how difficult it is to treat certain conditions with allopathic or "Western" medicines when the case cannot be correctly diagnosed. This can still be true today, in spite of the many truly amazing advances in Western medicine and technology.

Case History: Captain Abdul Kader

During the year 1972, I cut my left ankle, near a vein, with a rusty spade. There was no bleeding or swelling in the area and only a little pain that subsided after the application of penicillin ointment.

During 1973, after a tiring game of tennis, I had severe pain and swelling on the left ankle where I'd cut myself with the spade. My doctor advised complete bed rest, a support bandage and a Tenderil tablet three times a day. The pain and swelling both disappeared after three days, but the vein under the affected area — for a length of approximately two centimeters — had thickened like a steel-wire rope and the color had changed to almost dark blue. However, since there was no more pain or swelling I did not consult the doctor again.

During May of 1974 after a long training march, the swelling and severe pain began again along the same vein between the left ankle and knee. A surgical specialist performed a biopsy on the thickened vein and diagnosed thrombo-phlebitis. I was given a heavy dose of strepto-penicillin injections and the problem subsided. By then, however, I could feel that the bluish thickened vein extended all the way from my ankle to my knee.

In September of that year, I felt a mild pain in the left thoracic region which I mistook for the effects of a cough and cold. But in October, I experienced severe chest pain, sweating, and difficulty in breathing and fell down unconscious. I was evacuated to the army hospital in Delhi where I was told it was probably a pulmonary embolism in my left lung, combined with a partially blocked artery to the heart.

While in the hospital, a mild pain started in my left forearm, followed by two pea-sized swellings. After about a month, the two swellings coalesced to form a diffused swelling. A biopsy from this area confirmed thrombophlebitis migrans.

From 1974 on I was given periodic allopathic treatments by eminent doctors in some six hospitals. These treatments were mainly heavy doses of antibiotics and long-term intravenous and oral anticoagulants which gave me short-term relief from complaints pertaining to thrombo-phlebitis migrans. I was also advised to stop smoking and not exert myself physically, as the existing clots could move into any part of my body and result in instantaneous death or severe disability.

Having known from experts that no curative medicines were available for thrombo-phlebitis, I consulted Mrs. Chakravarti. She gave me 18 sittings of "vibration therapy" — one sitting per day for twenty to thirty minutes. This gave me instantaneous relief. What is more, I could feel that the thickened veins had become soft and that the clots were dissolving. Pulsations that were absent in the lower limbs resumed after just a few sittings.

By the end of her treatments, my electro-cardiogram had returned to normal. The clots had dissolved and since then no further clots have been detected in my veins. I am once again exerting myself like any healthy person and have no complaints of thrombo-phlebitis.

This unusual treatment administered by Mrs. Chakravarti is a challenge to the regular medical profession and to allopathic doctors who claim to be second only to God. May God bless her with a long life that can be devoted to the service of ailing humanity.

— Captain Abdul Kader
Delhi, India
18 February, 1977

I continue to treat various problems associated with thrombo-phlebitis successfully. Something in the vibration of my hand plus the natural cures I recommend appear to be effective in these cases.

Herbal Remedies For Thrombo-Phlebitis

I chiefly recommend that patients drink at least eight glasses of water daily, plus the liquid obtained by soaking *kulthi gram* overnight in water to improve the blood's circulation and because it slowly lowers cholesterol. If *kulthi* is not available, patients with cholesterol problems could try drinking the water from soy beans and chick peas soaked overnight.

I also recommend that once daily my patients chew 15-20 freshly washed *tulsi* leaves and swallow the juice. This acts as a general tonic in addition to improving the circulation of the blood. For more information about *kulthi gram*, *tulsi* leaves, and soy bean/chick pea treatments, please see Part 2, Chapter 23, "Herbal and Natural Remedies."

Massaging Your Big Toes To Keep Your Brain Alert

I strongly recommend a simple but very important foot reflexology exercise for keeping the mind alert and the brain healthy: massaging each of your big toes daily to keep blood flowing to your brain. This is because the nerve endings for the carotid arteries of the neck that carry blood to the brain are in the big toes. Imagine that each inner side of your big toes represents your neck: the inside of the left toe has the nerve endings of the neck's left carotid artery; the inside of the right toe has the nerve endings for the neck's right carotid artery

To do this exercise, grasp and hold each of your big toes in turn between your thumb and forefinger. Press hard on the inside of the big toe until you locate the tender area near the joint. For most people this joint area will be very tender to the touch; this may indicate that your carotid artery is silting up with cholesterol or it can be due to the body being very stiff.

Massage the tender area for a few seconds, then placing your thumb and forefinger on either side of your big toe, push them firmly from the base to the top at least five or six times. This massage will increase the flow of blood to the brain, improve the glandular function and help your mind to remain alert.

It's a good idea to use a little vegetable oil or lotion on the toes when you are doing this exercise to avoid skin abrasions.

Heart Problems

Throughout my book I mention a number of different forms of heart weakness that I've been able to treat successfully. My earliest cases were the child with a hole in her heart and the major-general with a career-threatening heart murmur. Over the years I have also treated various other forms of heart weakness such as palpitations and cholesterol sedimentation, as well as cases where heart problems have been misdiagnosed.

As in the case of blood clots, the vibration of my hand seems to be effective in many heart cases. I also sometimes recommend an Indian ayurvedic medicine, *Abana*®, that has helped regulate and stabilize the heart in several cases I've treated.

One of my recent patients, Kamal Maettle, is a young and successful New Delhi industrialist who received his engineering and management training at the Massachusetts Institute of Technology in the United States. I originally treated him for spinal problems and he has written his case history for my book.

Case History: Kamal Maettle

I first met Mrs. Chakravarti when I was suffering from excruciating pain in my back from a bone pressing on a nerve. When painkillers, medicines, and rest did me no good, I finally allowed an uncle to arrange an appointment with the spiritual healer he spoke of in such glowing terms. All my scientific training made me intensely skeptical.

On my first visit I went up the two flights of stairs to Mrs. Chakravarti's flat with great difficulty. She struck me immediately as a very simple person with no ego or airs about her. Meeting her husband, Colonel Chakravarti, for many years an army man and a scholar of Hindu philosophy and Sanskrit, also gave me a lot of confidence.

I lay down on the treatment bed and Mrs. Chakravarti's fingers very soon found the place on my back that felt like a half-inch hole. When she touched it gently her hand started vibrating or one could say, fluttering. Her hand's vibrations stopped spontaneously after fifteen or twenty minutes and I found I could walk much more easily. With no rational explanation possible, it was hard for me to believe this had actually happened.

For the next several weeks I went to see Mrs. Chakravarti twice a week. Gradually this particular spot on my back shrank to the size of a pinhead and then completely disappeared. With my scientific background, it was difficult to explain this healing process logically, but there is nothing like actually feeling it happen! My feeling was, Who cares if it works. *Didi* ("Elder sister" as we now call her) also gave me a lot of love.

A year later I again had a problem with my back. Instead of going straight to *Didi*, I started seeing medical specialists. Somehow I had felt her treatment might have worked earlier because my condition had been less serious, and that it could not work this time. My medical file became inches thick. One specialist at the All India Institute of Medical Sciences — a premier institute — was surprised I wasn't in intensive care. After several weeks of this, my wife begged me to go to *Didi*. On my first visit to her I felt better and again she cured me, something the specialists had given up on.

I had by now developed a strong bond with *Didi* and her husband, and my wife had also started seeing her. I wanted to tell her whole world about *Didi*, but she told me she would only have too many people to treat. I could see she was already giving so much time to so many different kinds of people and all for love. She never takes a penny or a gift from anyone.

Then, in 1989 I had an attack of atrial fibrillation of the heart. I used to get feelings of blacking out and had to spend several days in the intensive care unit of the Heart Institute. My wife and I just grabbed hold of *Didi* like a lifeline. Several times I was sure I was close to my end, but *Didi* was always there keeping up our morale, and it is due to her treatment and moral support that I have a normal healthy life again.

If I let myself, I would be running to *Didi* with every little ailment, but I know she has more important things to do. God has chosen her for something very special in this world. We can only stand back and watch this great miracle worker and wonder at the mysterious and wonderful ways of the Almighty, for hers is indeed a gift straight from God. There is no other rational explanation.

— Kamal Maettle
New Delhi, India
1992

One strange incident took place in connection with my ability to diagnose heart problems. I was helping our servant Mungal Singh prepare lunch when we received a call from one of the disciples of a famous guru. "Baba _____ wishes to offer *darshan* (pay his respects) to Mother. Will Mother accept?" the disciple asked my husband. Of course my husband could not refuse, so he called out to me, "Better go change your sari, Baba and his disciples will never believe you are the 'Holy Mother' if they find you cutting up chicken!"

A little while later a fleet of fine cars — Mercedes Benz, Rolls Royce and the like — drew up at our door and our whole drawing room was like a party of fashionably dressed men and women. When I didn't see the guru among them, I went to the door and found him hunched over at the top of the marble stairs, his head in his hands, obviously unwell. He was dressed in a stained saffron shirt and his long oiled hair hung in tangles to his shoulders. He would not look up and greet me. Finally I persuaded him to come in and sit on a chair, but still he would not meet my eyes. My niece, who was there helping me, said why didn't I give him my healing touch, but my husband whispered to me in Bengali not to touch him, he looked too dirty. How could I not help him when he had come to offer me *darshan*, I replied. I brought a small cane stool and sat right in front of the guru so that he had to meet my eyes.

The minute I put my hand on his head, the guru told me that he used to heal people himself, but that today he had come to me for help. When I put my hand on his heart, I got very frightened. "Why have you come here?" I asked, "You must know you are having a major heart attack?"

"I know," he said, "I have come here to die in this holy place." With that he went and lay down on one of our sofas. I told him he would do no such thing and I made his disciples take him immediately to the best heart hospital in one of their big cars.

I felt sure he could not live, but a few hours later we got a call to say by the grace of God he had got there just in time and was recovering. Only later did I learn that Baba _____ was known to engage in the negative side of yoga, calling up the dark spirits to assist him in using the powers that gave him ascendancy over his followers. Then I knew why he had refused to meet my eyes until I forced him to. He knew that his power was evil and that my power came from God.

Diet and Herbal Remedies for Heart Patients

The diet I recommend to my heart patients is to follow the Golden Rule — moderation in everything. I also always tell my heart patients to consult their own heart doctors for their suggestions.

However, there *are* a few absolutes I advise on diet:

- Most heart patients need to lose weight, and this will happen naturally if they eat moderately.
- There is no doubt that heart patients must give up smoking in any form.
- Heart patients must give up or cut down on their consumption of alcohol, limiting their intake to not more than two small drinks a day.
- Heart patients should not eat red meat.

For herbal and natural cures I recommend the following:

- *Amlaki,* a fruit rich in iron and Vitamin C.
- Bark of *Arjun:* an herbal remedy that acts like a tonic.
- *Kulthi* water to reduce high blood pressure, lower the cholesterol level and generally cleanse the blood.
- *Tulsi* leaves to act as a general tonic and improve circulation of the blood.

I also sometimes recommend an ayurvedic medicine, *Abana*®, which I have found to be effective in helping heal many cases of heart weakness. *Abana*® can be bought at chemist shops without prescription in India, and is also often recommended to their heart patients by Indian doctors.

I also recommend eating the following vegetables for heart problems:

- Garlic and onions to help reduce arteriosclerosis (hardening of the arteries).
- Cabbage juice to help cleanse the intestinal tract.
- Spinach juice to help improve the heart functions and effect blood pressure changes.

Please see Part 2, Chapter 23, "Herbal and Natural Cures" for more information on these herbs, vegetables and the ayurvedic medicine, *Abana*®.

12
THE FRIEDRICH BAUR-STIFTUNG HOSPITAL IN MUNICH

A very rich man came to me one day for treatment of an acute inflammation caused by shingles (*herpes zoster*). It was through this meeting that I was invited to Germany to demonstrate my healing at the Friedrich Baur-Stiftung Hospital in Munich.

This man is now a great friend of mine, but initially we got off to a bad start. It is my custom not to go to a person's home unless they are too ill to come to me. This is because I find it drains too much of my energy to leave my own home to give a treatment. Sometimes when I have been out to see a patient, particularly if I have had to visit someone in hospital, I have no strength even to lift the iron latch on our garden gate when I return home.

When I heard that a very rich patient was asking me to come to him I thought, mistakenly, that he was a typical spoiled rich man used to getting his own way. I sent a message that I would treat him if he came to my clinic. He was insulted and thought I had refused to treat him. As it turned out, he truly was too ill to leave his house and when he eventually did come to me, I was very sorry to see him in such a pitiable state. He could not even lift his hands as the upper part of his body was afflicted with the herpes blisters. "Of course I would have come to your house if I had known how ill you are," I apologized.

I took a long time to cure the shingles and we became very good friends during his treatment. Later when he went to Germany on business, he visited the Friedrich Baur-Stiftung Hospital in Munich for a check-up and told the head of the hospital, Professor Bodechtel, how I had healed him. The professor was so interested that my patient arranged for them to invite me to Germany to demonstrate my healing to the doctors in the hospital.

It is very difficult to work in a foreign country where one does not speak the language, and with doctors who are all very eminent. However my friend and former patient was there to look after me and encourage me.

In the beginning the doctors and staff of the hospital were very hostile to me. They asked me to work only on patients who had been damaged in surgery. I wondered what I could do when the doctors had already caused the damage, but I did my best to restore flexibility to the patients' muscles.

I asked to see patients with serious back problems that had not yet been operated on, but Professor Bodechtel refused. He always introduced me as "the lady with the fantastic therapy." Every day he kept insisting that I teach a few of the doctors my "therapy." I kept telling them I had not learnt my "therapy" from anyone, that my healing powers were a gift. To the end of my visit, they were sure I had been taught by some guru in the Himalayas and was keeping my secrets from them.

I worked on a lot of the cases with one particular young doctor. He himself suffered from spondylitis and I gave him several treatments. When he heard I was going back to India, he begged me, "at least teach my wife your technique." I really did not know how to convince them I had a gift, not a method I could pass on. I had no idea I'd been invited to work with them just to teach them — if I'd known, I would have refused the invitation.

In the end I spent a month at the hospital. Slowly my methods started showing results. By the time I went home, everyone at the hospital had become much more cordial towards me.

When I returned from Germany, more and more people had come to know about me and I started handling increasingly serious and unusual cases. Many of these patients were sent by our own friends or family.

Previously many of them had not believed in my gift, but when they learned I had been asked to practice my healing at a famous German hospital by a famous German doctor, they thought surely I must have something. I didn't take to this sudden interest too kindly. It was as if I'd gone to Germany to get some kind of medical degree. My husband didn't say too much about this sudden interest by his family in my work, but he too became more cooperative and interested in my healing.

13
CURING KIDNEY AND SPINAL PROBLEMS

During the years that I have been healing, I have treated more kidney cases than any other health problem. I have found that doctors frequently do not detect a kidney problem, even when they study the kidneys by injecting dye into the bloodstream. Of course doctors often do discover kidney stones, kidney infections, and kidney failures, but I have been surprised how many times my hand vibrates over the kidneys when the doctor has diagnosed the patient as having spinal, heart, or gastric problems. Perhaps I am able to find kidney problems more easily because I follow the holistic theory of medicine. I treat the whole person — body, mind and spirit — not just one part at a time.

I have also found that many patients are not told how antibiotics and other often essential treatments may damage the kidneys, and how they can take simple precautions like flushing out the system by drinking lots of water. However from experience I know that if my recommendations are followed, most kidney problems can be permanently cured.

I have put kidney cures and healing spinal problems together in this chapter as, in my experience, kidney problems so often contribute to or are misdiagnosed as spinal problems. Also the diet I recommend, particularly the need to drink a lot of water, is good for both conditions. For the kidneys, frequent drinks of water will help flush out toxins. For the spine, water helps to achieve spinal flexibility.

A Regimen for Kidney Patients

I have put the regimen I recommend to kidney patients up front because I refer to it so often in this chapter when discussing cases I have cured. The dietary restrictions would apply equally well to patients with spinal problems.

Basic to the system I recommend is that patients with kidney problems should do the following:

- Eat no red meat.
- Drink at least 8 glasses of water a day.
- Take plenty of watermelon and cucumber juices. If they can be taken in conjunction with the herb *kanta gokhur*, they will be even more effective.
- Avoid tea and coffee as both tea and coffee harden the kidneys.
- Try to avoid raw tomatoes, raw onions, and cooked spinach.
- In addition, and very important, I strongly advise drinking the water in which *kulthi* grain has been soaked.

Kulthi (dolichos bifiorus) is grown all over India, but some of the best of this grain comes from the mountains of the Kulu Valley where it is a regular item in the local people's daily diet. In the south of India, stone carvers soak the stone they will be working on in *kulthi* water to soften it. *Kulthi* water can be drunk safely each day. It acts to flush out the kidneys and keep them healthy. If taken in conjunction with an ayurvedic medicine, Turaico®, affected kidneys will be cured more swiftly.

For patients with kidney stones, *kulthi* water will help dissolve them in conjunction with Cystone®, another ayurvedic medicine I recommend. *Kulthi* water is also effective in reducing the cholesterol count and, because it is a natural diuretic, in lowering high blood pressure.

- For nephritis (chronic inflammation of the kidney): one teaspoon of ginger powder mixed with any food and taken once daily helps cure this kidney ailment.
- For bladder weakness: For problems of urine retention, take 1 teaspoon of onion juice daily.
- As a kidney cleanser: drink parsley juice daily.

For more information on the preparation of *kulthi* and *kanta gokhur* and information about the ayurvedic medicines Cystone® and Turaico®, please see Part 2, Chapter 23, "Herbal and Natural Remedies."

A Regimen for Patients with Spinal Problems

The dietary recommendations given above for kidney patients apply equally well to patients with spinal problems, since the prime need of patients with spinal problems is to achieve spinal flexibility. Cystone® and Turaico®, of course should *only* be taken if a kidney problem is involved. In addition, I recommend the following treatments for spinal problems.

- Applications of Father Causaunal's plaster, a healing compress.
- Applications of heated rock salt.
- Practice of two *asanas* (yoga body exercises): the *sarpa asana* (serpent posture) and an *asana* I invented myself for patients with spinal problems.

Please see Chapter 23 for information on Father Causaunal's plaster and heated rock salt, and Chapter 25 for information on the two *asanas*.

Some Unusual Kidney Cases

When I returned from Germany one of my first patients was a young Saudi Arabian boy whose father was working at the Saudi Embassy. The boy was suffering from hematuria (blood in the urine) and whenever he passed water he screamed with pain. The parents had tried many doctors, including London's Harley Street specialists. The boy had been put through all the tests, but the doctors could only suggest the boy would probably "grow out of" his affliction.

When I checked him I found my hand was vibrating a lot over both kidneys. I explained to the parents that their son would need several sittings and that they must be sure he followed the regimen I prescribed very strictly. I was able to cure the boy with a combination of diet and my hand vibrations. Within a few weeks he stopped passing blood and started to put on weight. When I went to Saudi Arabia a few months later the boy had completely recovered.

I particularly remember one patient who was brought to see me just before he was due for spinal surgery. A famous orthopedic surgeon in Bombay had already set the date for the operation. I only saw the man for a second opinion at the insistence of a good friend who had tremendous faith in the diagnostic power of my right hand, and was hoping his friend could avoid the complicated surgery. But I was sure he must need spinal surgery if such an eminent surgeon was involved.

The patient was an unusually tall man, and when he walked into our house the first thing I noticed about him was how he kept bending over to one side every few minutes. Looking up at him I said straight out, "It seems pointless for me to check you if the operation is already scheduled by such a famous doctor. But tell me, I am interested in why you keep bending over like that."

"My spine gets so stiff I can only walk if I bend over every few steps to stretch it," he told me.

When I checked him with my right hand I was amazed to find he had absolutely nothing wrong with his spine. "Your vertebrae column is perfect," I said, "but one of your kidneys has shrunk. Tell me what you normally eat and drink."

I was not too surprised to learn that he drank very little water. He told me he drank tea all day and also ate a lot of raw tomatoes, raw onions, and cooked spinach. I recommended he drink plenty of water, including *kulthi* water, and that he avoid tomatoes, onions, and cooked spinach. He followed my advice and with the diet and a few of my treatments he became completely cured. He never had to have the operation and has been perfectly well since.

I first met Shalini Kumar when she was being treated for a slipped disc which also turned out to be mainly a kidney problem. I had to visit her at home as she had been in such acute pain she had not been able to get out of bed for two months.

When I walked into her bedroom I found a pretty young woman surrounded by all the pulleys, ropes, and weights for traction treatment. When I examined her, I found there was some curvature of the spine, but no slipped disc. My hand vibrated for a long time over her kidneys. Both kidneys were very hard. When I asked if she had any history of urinary problems, she told me that over the previous ten years she had had several severe urinary infections.

When I looked around the comfortable bedroom I noticed she was sleeping directly in front of a "desert cooler," which blows water-cooled air into the room. "How long has your bed been in that position?" I asked her. She told me it had been there for two months, just the period that her back problem had become acute.

"You must change the position of your bed and never expose your back to a direct draft," I advised. By the time I finished my first treatment, she was able to get up and walk a little on her own. I have continued over the years to treat her for urinary problems, but her back problem has never recurred. Shalini describes her case in her own words:

Case History: Shalini Kumar

I shall never forget my first memory of Sree when she came to see me about eight o'clock one evening in April 1986. She looked so different from anyone I knew — dignified and some special aura about her with the big red *tikka* mark on her forehead.

Ever since the birth of my third child — all three by caesarian — I had had some back problem or other. By February of that year the pain had become unbearable and I had gone on homeopathic medicines after trying all sorts of painkillers. Suddenly one day in March I could hardly walk back to my car after shopping and only with the greatest difficulty came home. My husband consulted the top orthopedic doctors and got different opinions. Finally in April one of the doctors was sure that I had a slipped disc and put me in traction — with weights of over 15 kilograms. Before this I had tried many sittings with diathermy, but got only temporary relief. Anyway, nothing helped and I was in absolute despair.

One day my husband's cousin came from Madras and told me his sister knew of a lady who could help me. That same evening his sister walked into my room with *Didi* ("elder sister") as I now call Sree. Sree asked me to get up and I kept insisting that it was too painful. Finally with a lot of effort I managed to stand, half bent. *Didi* put her hand on my back to diagnose my problem and told me not to tell her where the pain was. Within half a minute her hand went right to the painful part and after making me lie down, she gave me her vibrations for almost 45 minutes. It was painful at that moment, but at the same time I felt great relief. Then she asked me to walk just a few steps around the room, and I did, after so many weeks!

The next three weeks (I would stay in our car the first week) I went to *Didi's* home about 10 to 12 times. She would give me at least 30 to 40 minutes each time and within 10 days I was walking in the house, and about six weeks later I went for a holiday to the hills. Our friends were amazed that I was fit enough to go, but I had a wonderful week there. By being a little careful, my back remained fine and I followed *Didi's* instructions about drinking a lot of water because she diagnosed not a slipped disc but poor functioning of the kidneys. She asked me whether I had had any urinary infections and I told her that I had had urinary troubles even since the birth our second child. *Didi* felt that the many infections I'd had, and not flushing out the kidneys properly with water, had aggravated my back problems.

About a year later I started getting the same pain in the other side, and again took bed rest for a few days. We were to go on a pilgrimage to the temple of Vaishna Devi in Jammu which involved 12 kilometers of hard walking and climbing to reach the shrine and 12 kilometers back, all in one day. As usual, I ran to *Didi*, and in just four sittings I felt so much better that a week later I was able to make the pilgrimage. Just as a precaution I wore a surgical belt, but I had no problems at all.

It is almost six years now, and by being a little careful, I feel just fine. *Didi* and I have become so close that she has filled the gap of losing my mother. I know *Didi* will always be there when I need her.

— Shalini Kumar
New Delhi, India
1992

I have also cured slipped discs by treating the kidneys in addition to vibrating my hand on the spine. One patient was a Saudi man who had worked for many years at the United Nations in New York. He had been hospitalized there, but had found no permanent relief.

When I examined him in Delhi, I found he did have a disc problem, but that his kidneys were also very hard, perhaps from all the painkillers he had been taking. I told him about drinking *kulthi* water and also asked him not to drink too much tea or coffee as caffeine hardens the kidneys. I also gave him special exercises to do, based on yoga.

By drinking a lot of water, his body became much more flexible and one day he felt his disc slip back into place while doing the *sarpa asana* (serpent posture) and a posture I devised myself. When he came to see me, I asked him why he didn't look happier. "I am sure the disc will slip out of place again," he said.

"I've treated many disc cases and none of the patients have ever come back with the same problem," I reassured him. When I later visited Saudi Arabia, he came to see me, looking very slim and fit. The *sarpa asana* and my exercise are described in Chapter 25.

One patient who *did* have his back trouble recur was visiting India and did not have time for as many treatments as he needed. He also did not take sensible precautions. My friend Deepak Kapoor explains below what happened to him when he returned home.

Case History: Deepak Kapoor

In early 1988, when I was visiting India, a very close family member extracted a promise from me to see Mrs. Sree Chakravarti about my chronic back problem, a problem that had persisted since 1983 and had become quite unmanageable since early 1986. I must admit that until I was actually treated by Mrs. Chakravarti, I thought the whole idea of seeing someone who allegedly healed by touch would be a total waste of time.

As ridiculous as I thought the whole idea was, I made the appointment and visited Sree Chakravarti. I was asked to wait in her living room as she was busy with another patient. After a few minutes she came into the room and without any idea why I was there she asked me to turn my back to her and her hand went immediately to the epicenter of my pain — a spot which had escaped high-tech scans (CAT, MRI) and a score of orthopedic specialists and neurologists. With the minimum of words, I was taken to another room and asked to lie face down on a small mattress. All she did was touch the spot and the area around it, covering an area of not more than a few inches in every direction from the center of the pain, only for a few minutes. During those brief moments an enormous amount of electrical (or that's what it seemed to be) energy passed through my entire body. The center of pain was thoroughly agitated with the mere touch of her fingers — no pressure, no other devices, no lotions.

When I stood up it felt as if years of ever-present pain had been drained away. That day I could jump up and touch the ceiling. Beginning that same night, I started sleeping properly.

My skepticism had been replaced by total belief.

Unfortunately, my confidence was so much enhanced that when I got home to Florida I moved a full-sized refrigerator and hurt myself again. Sree had warned me at the outset that I needed several more treatments and that I should be careful since I did not have time to stay and see her again. Through the years I have come to know her and appreciate her work a good deal more than on my first visit. The efficacy of her work is beyond question. On top of that she refuses to accept any money or even gifts from anyone. Quite often she spends her own money to dispense some medication. She is a wonderful person and that might explain why God has blessed her with the special gift of healing.

> — Deepak Kapoor
> Melbourne, Florida,
> U.S.A.
> 1992

Another slipped disc patient with a kidney problem was a very famous pathologist from the All India Institute of Medical Science. He was brought to my house in great pain and the first thing he said was, "My surgeon friend wants to put me in a total body cast, he says that's the only way I'll get well."

When I examined him my hand confirmed the disc problem, but I also found that one kidney was very hard. "I think I can cure you if you follow my instructions very carefully," I told him. I gave his back a few treatments with my hand, prescribed *kulthi* water for his kidney, and his slipped disc was completely cured.

Some years later, this same pathologist again came to me. "You told me my slipped disc would never come back, well it has," he reproached me. He was very upset as he was due to leave in a few days for an important assignment in Afghanistan. "Do you think you can possibly cure me in time?"

"How did the problem start this time?" I asked.

"Very slowly, not like the time before," he told me. I know this is not common in slipped disc cases. When I checked him, I found that one kidney was again very hard.

"It's not your back, it's your kidney that's the problem," I told him. After three treatments and drinking *kulthi* water, he was perfectly fit for Afghanistan.

Another interesting kidney patient was a German man stationed in Delhi for Lufthansa Airlines who came to see me because he had the strange feeling that his fingers were shrinking. If he drank any alcohol it felt worse. He had been to a lot of doctors, but none of them had been able to give him any idea of what was wrong with him. As usual, one of my first questions was, "How much water do you drink?"

"None," he said firmly, "I am very careful to avoid drinking water in India, I take only coffee."

"It is perfectly safe for your health to drink boiled water in India, and you need to drink water here," I told him. "The climate is very different from Germany. Our body is 70 percent fluid and we need seven to eight glasses a day in our hot weather to replace lost body fluid." I prescribed *kulthi* water to flush out his kidneys and he telephoned in a few days to say he was feeling much better. I told him to slowly reduce his intake of coffee and, whenever he did drink coffee, to drink a little water first.

Another unusual case also concerned the effects of caffeine. A young man came to me one day with his mother to see if I could diagnose his problem. He had tremors in both hands but, after putting him through all the tests, the doctors were no wiser. When I checked him my hand vibrated quite a lot on his head and I felt somehow it was related to excessive drinking. "Does he take alcohol?" I asked his mother privately. She assured me he only drank an occasional beer. Then I asked what his job involved. The young man told me he was a tea taster and had to sip some two hundred cups of tea a day.

"It's the tannin in the tea that is affecting your nervous system," I told him.

"But I only take one sip from each cup," he protested.

"Even so, I strongly advise you to change your job if you hope to recover," I told him. I treated his head until my hand stopped vibrating and I have not heard from him since.

A very recent patient, Martin Howard, came to me for a long-standing problem with his kidney, but I was also able to help him with a jaw injury he'd received some forty years before I met him. He has kindly written his case history for my book.

Case History: Martin Howard

After thirty-five years in the Royal Navy, with a number of years as air crew for whom fitness and rigorous annual medicals are the order of the day, I joined the commercial world in 1988. I had spent the last four years of my naval career in India, and in March 1990 Rolls-Royce took me on as the Indian Sub-continent resident regional executive, from which time we have lived in Delhi again.

In December 1991 I had two molar teeth in my right lower jaw filled. After four days I developed a sharp pain in that part of the jaw when I opened my mouth. In a few more days the pain had become excessive and I could open my jaw no more than a quarter of an inch and that only with difficulty. My dentist said that it was a muscle spasm, most likely brought on by strenuous work, triggered by the interference of the injection he had applied. He advised me to rest the jaw as much as possible, but with Christmas in England coming up that would not be an easy task.

The next day we flew to the United Kingdom where I immediately consulted my homeopath who diagnosed through iridology that my third cervical vertebra appeared inflamed.

In addition to giving me some helpful pills, he recommended I consult an osteopath. I did, and after a few massages of the upper vertebrae and the right jaw and head muscles, things improved and I came back to India. During the osteopathic consultation, I recalled that nearly forty years earlier at Dartmouth, while boxing, I had taken a hefty blow on the left side of my jaw. It had given me some pain which cleared up after a while, but I had never since been able to open my mouth very wide. About a year later, a troublesome aching tooth had had to be taken out, but the dentist said that there was nothing wrong with it. At that time I did not connect the aching tooth with the blow to my jaw, finding a possible connection only when pressed by the osteopath so many years later.

Then came Sree. I heard about her from my good friend Menakshi Matoo. All my life I had perceived a weakness in my kidneys; if I am to get a cold or even other complaints, the attacks are almost always heralded by a feeling that I have let my back get cold, followed by aching knees. I asked Menakshi if she would put me in touch with Sree to fix my kidneys, but I mentioned my jaw problem also. I was now convinced that there was some irregularity which might cause future problems, stemming from my boxing injury.

On my first visit to Sree I could hardly bear her touching my kidneys, they were so tender. I was amazed at the uncanny speed and accuracy with which she could put her finger on the very tenderest spot. She did her gentle search and brief massage followed by vibratory treatment with her right hand.

On my jaw, she again went straight to the most sensitive spot and probed around before vibrating with her right hand. She treated my upper vertebrae which were still stiff and painful and my scalp because of headaches. She also treated the area around my right shoulder blade, as the pain from my jaw had migrated over a number of weeks into my neck and now lay in that shoulder blade area.

Over a period of five weeks, with a break for one week while I was out of Delhi, I visited Sree seven or eight times, at the end of which her hand vibrated no more and all the pain, and the headaches as well, had gone.

So far my kidneys have given me no reason to suspect them and they are certainly less sensitive to being uncovered, and I can now open my jaw wider than I have been able to since that boxing blow at Dartmouth.

— Martin Howard
New Delhi, India
1992

I recently had an unusual case, a fourteen year old girl suffering from a supposedly incurable disease in which the body fat slowly wastes away.

I told her parents I had never heard of the disease. They showed me places on her body where there were dents like dimples where the fat had wasted. One place in her leg was particularly soft. When I put my hand on these "dimples" there was only a very mild vibration. I knew the cause must be somewhere else. I checked her kidneys and found both were very hard.

When I asked the parents if she had ever suffered from any kidney problems, they told me she had had many attacks. Typically she got a high temperature and passed pus cells, blood, and albumin.

I checked the young girl's kidneys once a week for several months while the parents made her follow my diet very strictly, drink lots of water and *kulthi* water and also take the ayurvedic medicine, Turaico®. The "dimples" had almost filled in when my hand stopped vibrating on her kidneys. I told the parents I had done all I could and they must take very good care of the girl's kidneys for the rest of her life.

Within a few months they returned. They had not kept up the *kulthi* water and Turaico®, the girl was running a low fever and she had an obvious dent in her nose. Again I started treating her and this time they kept strictly to my recommendations. Again the "dimples" disappeared and I warned them that they must realize that this had to be a lifetime regimen.

Transferring my Healing Power to Water

One rather different case that also involved the kidneys was that of a woman who'd been thrown from a jeep when the axle had broken. She had injured her spine and broken both legs. She was in acute pain and I had to visit her in the hospital. I was surprised to learn she could actually feel the vibration of my hand through the plaster cast and was in less pain after my visits.

During her treatment she was given so many drugs and pain killers that both her kidneys had hardened and she was having a lot of trouble passing urine. As I could not go to the hospital each day, I started sending her water to drink that I had treated with my hand. The patient drank the water I treated each day and her urinary problem was solved.

When I plunge my hand into water, some of the healing energy in my hand is transferred to the water. When I first put my hand into the water, it foams up around my hand. If I put my hand in a moment later, the water remains still. The water will keep its healing power as long as it does not touch metal, so I always had to do this in a plastic or glass container, and the water was taken to a patient in a plastic or glass container.

I discovered I had this gift by accident, and I used to practice it quite a lot until an astrologer told me it would take away too much of my healing power. He also told me that I must not use my water-divining skills — which I discovered I had in Germany with a German water diviner — because water for me was a negative force.

The Importance of Drinking Water

As anyone reading this chapter knows, I am a great believer in the curative powers of drinking water. No one should ever underestimate the power of plain water as an cleansing and healing agent for the whole system.

I almost invariably find that people who come to me with kidney problems do not drink enough water, and it is always one of the first things I recommend to them, in addition to the use of *kulthi* water.

I am frequently asked by patients, "But I drink a lot of tea (or coffee). That's liquid, isn't that just as good as water?"

"Would you take a bath in tea or coffee?" is the answer I give. The caffeine in tea and coffee acts to harden the kidneys. Water flushes them out and is the most effective remedy open to all of us.

For myself, I drink water constantly all day because I try very hard to protect my healing gift by keeping my own body as healthy as possible.

14
A ROYAL INVITATION TO SAUDI ARABIA

In 1972, at the end of April, I was invited by the then Prime Minister of Saudi Arabia, Prince Fahd, to visit Riyadh and Jeddah in Saudi Arabia and also Egypt and Beirut. I would be treating a number of special patients, including Prince Fahd himself. The invitation was delivered in person by Enus Yasin, the Saudi Arabian ambassador to India. This visit turned out to be one of the most interesting few weeks of my life.

Initially, there were a lot of problems. My husband was also invited, but he did not wish to come as I had been invited as a healer. We didn't realize that Saudi visas, at that time anyway, were not given to women traveling alone. When the ambassador explained, I had to tell him my husband would not change his mind. "Either I go alone, or I don't go," I said.

More problems arose. As friends heard about the invitation, they told my husband all sorts of stories that made him more and more worried. Without his express approval, I would never go. Finally my husband spoke to friends at the External Affairs Ministry. They assured him it was a great honor to be invited, that the Saudis were extremely nice people, and I would be taken care of in a way few countries could afford to. He came home and told me to phone the ambassador and accept.

In spite of all the initial difficulties, I had always been sure I would go to Saudi Arabia in the end. This was because a few days before we'd received the invitation, I had had a vivid dream. In the dream an old man I do not recognize but who seems familiar is standing by a handcart, urging me to go to a certain, unspecified place. "I cannot go," I keep telling him. He keeps insisting and finally I sit in the handcart when he says he will take me there himself. I asked a friend to interpret the dream for me. "You will soon go out of India, and you will travel alone," he had told me. Then I knew I need not be afraid because Sai Baba would be with me. I had also consulted an astrologer who had told me I would be going to a Muslim country where "they will be benefited and you will be happy," he had said.

When I told the ambassador I could go, he was very relieved. I learned much later, when I was in Saudi Arabia, that a man had been sent especially to New Delhi to study me for a year before I'd been invited. He was to find out if I was really gifted, whether I took money for healing, whether I was of good character, treated more men than women, had a husband who took proper care of me, and so on. I also learned I was the only woman traveling alone to get a visa. When I heard all this I felt really very proud to think I'd been so honored.

To get to Riyadh I had to fly from New Delhi to Bombay to catch the plane for Saudi Arabia. I wanted to travel looking well dressed and I made the mistake of wearing a fine silk sari that became horribly crushed in the April heat. That gave me a good lesson in how often people judge by external appearances only.

When I boarded the plane in Bombay — small, hot and bedraggled — the Indian air hostess took one look at me and directed me to economy class. "But I have a first-class ticket," I told her. She was adamant, but very embarrassed when the next hostess escorted me back to my proper seat. When we arrived in Riyadh, the other first-class passengers pushed past me to the exit as someone not worthy of notice. I waited quietly to one side, but when the door opened, the Saudi Chief of Protocol stood there asking for me. A huge car, flags flying, was waiting for me at the bottom of the ramp. All the passengers looked at me in bewilderment — who is this woman looking like a schoolgirl, they must have wondered, but they made way for me very respectfully.

The Chief of Protocol, too, and the people with him looked surprised when they saw me. I asked them why. "We expected to meet an old lady,' they told me, "but instead we find we've come to meet a young lady." Perhaps next to their large and substantial forms I did look very young and tiny.

I was told that at the hotel I was to meet a cousin of King Faizal, who had come to Jeddah by the evening flight. I was a little nervous, but he turned out to be a very charming and friendly man. The hotel near the airport where I stayed had been the harem of the previous king and I had been given the best suite. Almost as soon as I arrived, the hotel manager came to tell me I should order whatever food I wanted. "Please, do not trouble too much, I will eat everything you cook, except beef," I told him.

The Chief of Protocol told me I had a car and driver at my disposal from morning until late at night. "Please do not go out without my permission," he warned me, "I am responsible for your safety." Before I left New Delhi I had been given a sealed envelope with the names of my first patients. "You will be given more names, and you must treat only those people. We have kept your visit a secret. If it becomes common knowledge, it will be difficult to control the crowds." I wondered to myself if perhaps they did not want it known that members of the royal family were being treated by a woman, and a woman of the Hindu religion. I didn't know then of the long tradition of woman healers in Arabia including Hafsa, the wife of Prophet Muhammad.

I remember very clearly my first visit to the palace of the Commander-in-Chief, Prince Abdullah, a famous horseman and a gentle, cultured man. His palace, like so many of the others I visited, was like a separate town, surrounded by high brick walls with huge iron gates set into them that opened only when the driver had spoken to the guard and obtained permission to enter. He explained I was the "Hakime Hind" ("Indian doctor") and the gates would swing open.

I had to talk to Prince Abdullah through my interpreter as he did not speak English. He was very interested in the large *tikka* mark on my forehead, why it was so much larger than the one most Indian ladies wore. "It's because I have such a large forehead," I said. Then he asked if we used *tikka* marks instead of lipstick. "No, it's to show a woman is married." One day he showed me a photo of himself carrying a child. I asked if the boy were his only son as he had so many other pictures of the same boy. "Of course not," he was very surprised, "I have many, many sons." All the princes had three official wives, who each had their own palaces.

I also treated the Crown Prince for heart problems in his huge palace, surprisingly modest considering he was next in succession. When King Faizal was shot dead I believe he became king for a short time until Prime Minister Prince Fahd was made king.

King Faizal's palace was the one I liked best. I used to visit the queen there most evenings. She was a very beautiful woman with modern ideas who spoke English fluently. I treated her for a problem with her fingers, and it was typical of her courtesy that she would always send one of her daughters to escort me when I washed my hands after treatment, never a maid. Each evening she would ask how I was, whether I was having to treat too many people. All her children had been well educated, unlike many of the other princesses I treated. One of her sons was a pilot.

At the time I was there, women lived a very restricted life compared to my life in India. No woman could go out without wearing the long black cloak called a *burka* that covers the head and face as well as the body. They were not allowed to drive. As there were no cinemas or restaurants, all the entertaining was in the home. At parties, men and women almost never sat in the same room.

I also found the laws very different, and unusually strict. I was told there was virtually no theft because if anyone was caught stealing, his right hand was cut off. Hangings were done in public and the body left for several days as an object lesson. If anyone killed someone while driving, relatives of the dead person had the option to kill the offender the same way.

I also treated Prince Fahd's wife and a very pretty daughter whose partial facial paralysis I was able to cure. One day Prince Fahd's wife and some of her friends asked me the secret of my slim body, since many of them were very overweight. "I can tell you," I said, "but you will probably get angry with me." They insisted, so I told them, "Wash your own clothes, sweep your own rooms."

"But how can we, when we have so many servants?" They were genuinely shocked. "At least try to sweep one room," I said. We all had a good laugh.

There were a very large number of servants in the palaces. I saw slaves, too, for the first time in Riyadh. I was told they had been bought when they were very young, but they were treated like regular servants and their children were no longer slaves. The problems of slavery linger on in some unexpected places. One day I was treating an important man's wife whose complexion was unusually dark. As is my custom after treatment, I washed my hand to clean and cool it. She was furious. "You are only doing that because I am so dark," she said. I had to explain to her husband that my hand becomes hot during treatment and I always wash it. He told me privately that she had an inferiority complex because she was the daughter of a black slave.

Saudi hospitality is truly legendary. One example is the Turkish coffee they serve. Wherever I went, I had to drink this coffee. A maid stands beside you with the coffee pot and the minute you put your cup down, she pours in just one more sip until you shake your cup to say "no more." I asked why they never served a full cup. "It would not be proper, the coffee would become cold, and it would mean we were tired of our guest," they told me. Another example is the amount of food cooked for each meal. Even if only a few people are invited, food is cooked for at least fifty with many, many different dishes. Sometimes I had to attend three dinner parties a night as I was told people would be insulted if I didn't go. But after working the whole day, I was often very tired.

My only other problem was purely logistical. Whenever I was to treat one of the princes, his car would come to the hotel. After treatment, I would have to return to the hotel and take a different prince's car, or my own car and driver. It was such a waste of time. Finally I had to say that, except for the few palaces I had visited from the beginning, the other princes must come to the hotel if they wanted to see me.

Somehow the news of my being there had spread all over and long queues of people waited outside the hotel to see me and ask me just to touch them. The Chief of Protocol told me to ignore them, but it made me feel sad not to be able to help. Originally, I had a few select patients; now I found I was working the whole day except for two hours rest in the afternoon. Then, when I went out in the evening, I would meet many ladies who begged me to treat them. Without telling the Chief of Protocol, I told them they could come to the hotel in the afternoon, when they could slip incognito through the entrance for women in their *burkas*.

One time I came home very late, about two o'clock in the morning. I'd been in bed half an hour when the phone rang. I heard a man's desperate voice asking if I was the Indian lady who cured people. "I am confined to my bed, please, please come and help me." I told him I was helpless, that I could only see patients arranged by the Chief of Protocol. He kept begging me and finally I had to put down the phone. I am still haunted by this man I could not help.

Today, when there is so much trouble between Hindus and Muslims in our country, I remember how in Saudi Arabia I never, even for one minute, felt I was someone different. I even went up to the last point in Mecca where non-Muslims are allowed to go, and when I was in Jeddah people used to walk long distances from Mecca just to see me. None of them worried that I was a Hindu, not a Muslim.

One of my last patients in Riyadh was a very large, very dark man with a slipped disc. An Indian friend had come to meet me and was surprised when he saw the enormous man come out of the room where I had been treating him. "Don't you feel afraid to treat such a big man alone in a room with the door closed?" he asked me.

"These good people consider me someone holy," I told him. "When I see such love and respect in their eyes, how can I feel unsafe? I find it much easier to treat someone like this than someone from Western society who has no idea of my noble work. I will always trust simple, God-fearing people, however strong they may look. They have come to seek help, and I am like a mother to that huge man."

After Riyadh I went to Jeddah for a short but eventful visit. While there, our Indian ambassador, T. T. K. Abdullah, looked after me. Unfortunately, the Chief of Protocol who had scheduled all my appointments in Riyadh had gone to Japan with King Faizal. The new protocol man did not understand I had to see patients more than once, that I could not see new people every day. Probably he had so many people asking for appointments, he could not refuse.

I would return for lunch to my hotel, very tired, sometimes as late as four P.M. One amusing thing was that every day a new hotel servant would bring me my meal — always they wanted me to help them. The crowds outside the hotel had now become almost unmanageable, and it was decided that between seeing my official patients, I would also treat some of these other people.

I remember one strange case in particular. This businessman was in such acute pain he would have to shut himself away in his room from his family so they would not see his agony. He had had his gall bladder and appendix removed, but nothing had helped. When I first saw him, I thought he was a very old man, his face was so lined. I doubted I could help him when so many doctors had failed, but on examination, I found some nerves had bundled together just above his diaphragm. He experienced immediate relief when my hand touched him. When he came next day, I actually did not recognize him, he looked so young and unwrinkled and smiling. After a few more treatments he was completely cured.

"You have returned me to my family, please allow me to entertain you at my home and meet them," he begged me. I went there for tea with our Indian ambassador and he presented the ambassador with a beautiful carpet. The ambassador wanted me to have it, but I told him I never accepted gifts for my healing. "You keep it," I told him, "and you will always remember how this man got cured."

One day in Jeddah I was treating a young boy for a slipped disc. My secretary came to tell me I must stop treating the boy because the Governor of Jeddah, Prince Mishal, was there to see me. "Please tell the prince I am with another patient, and to wait downstairs," I told her. She was very frightened and called in the man from protocol who ordered me to stop treating the boy.

"I am treating this boy by appointment," I told him. "The governor has no appointment. He must wait, and no one can stop me." At this point Prince Mishal came into the room, looking angry. I again told my secretary to ask him to wait in the other room. Speaking in Arabic, the protocol man told my secretary to tell the boy to leave. I could understand and lost my temper. "I am treating a case and I don't want to be disturbed, so you two get out of the room!"

Seeing me in a real temper, Prince Mishal said, "Maleesh, maleesh" ("Never mind, never mind") and he and the protocol man left the room quietly. The boy was very frightened and told me it was better for both of us if I stopped. I paid no attention and went on treating him. When it was time to go, he was so scared he couldn't tie his shoelaces. I told him not to be frightened, he was not the one to blame.

When he'd left, I told my secretary to call Prince Mishal from the other room. "You are a Saudi woman," I told her, "and you must translate what I say to this gentleman without changing a word." The prince told her gently and politely that he did not speak English, but he understood it very well.

"I must explain why I could not stop treating this boy," I said. "Once I start healing a person, the healing comes for that person, I never leave the case halfway. In my eyes, we are all, everyone of us, children of God, rich or poor. It is your luck, Prince Mishal, that you were born a prince. This boy was born poor, his destiny is to be your subject. I will stop treating people this way if you can show me that a drop of your blood is different from a drop of his. When I am treating you, if King Faizal should come and ask me to stop, I would not stop. So, now you know all the facts. If my behavior has offended you, I am really very sorry, and I ask your forgiveness."

"Please tell her I am very pleased with her reply," Prince Mishal told my secretary. "I would like her to come and have tea at my palace, and I would like to do something special for her." My secretary, knowing I would take nothing for myself, asked me to ask the prince if she and her husband could stay for some time rent-free at the house they were in that belonged to the prince. He immediately wrote them a chit for a year's free rent.

When I returned to India, I told the Saudi ambassador I hoped I had not offended Prince Mishal, in spite of his gracious behavior. "On the contrary, the prince told me he had never seen or met such a wonderful woman, she looks so delicate, but she possesses tremendous strength of character," was his reply.

The day I was to leave Jeddah, I had a very happy experience. The room bearer who took care of me each day always asked me what sort of talk I had had with Allah. "I am not so lucky to meet God," I would say, but he was a very simple man and did not believe me. The last day he told me that he had a very special *nawaj* (blessing) for me. All the workers in the hotel, some of whom I had treated, had said a special prayer for me. "This wonderful lady helps so many people and does not take anything for herself, but she is a human being and she must have some desire for something. Dear God, let her be given that desire without asking for it, that is our prayer."

I was choked with emotion and had tears in my eyes when I thanked him for this very special blessing. After this time, whenever I want something, it seems to come to me without my asking. Perhaps I will need to go somewhere and someone will come and ask to take me. Whenever something like this happens, I remember the servants in the hotel at Jeddah and their wonderful gift to me.

After Jeddah, I flew to Egypt where I treated special Saudi patients in Cairo and Alexandria. In Alexandria I stayed with the mother of the Saudi ambassador to India. He wanted me to treat his sister's sons, both of whom had muscular dystrophy. The disease sometimes runs in the family and, in fact, two other young boys related to them had died from it. I felt so sad not to be able to cure the boys, but I cannot help in any permanent way when all the cells of the body are affected.

After Alexandria I was flown to Beirut where I helped alleviate the heart trouble suffered by a famous doctor, the personal physician to King Faizal. They then wanted me to fly to London to treat another Saudi gentleman for spinal problems, but I had been out of India for two months already, and I told them I must return home.

Some ten years after I returned to New Delhi, a very interesting journalist, Margot Badran, visited India and through a patient of mine arranged to visit me. She wrote about her visit in the *Saudi Gazette* of May 16, 1981:

> Recently while in India I met a friend of mine, Shakuntala, who was glowing with health. The last time I had seen her she had been visibly unwell. Treatments by doctors and modern medicines had not been producing the intended effects. Noting my amazement at finding her so transformed, my friend promised to reveal the source of her cure.
>
> Late the following afternoon she drove me through the tree-lined streets of New Delhi, dappled in the bright reds and pinks of the luxuriant bougainvillea, to a house on a quiet street. We climbed up stairs to the second floor where a woman stood in the diminishing light of dusk. Shakuntala introduced me to Sree Chakravarti, a woman of the kind of exquisite simplicity that belies the extraordinary. Sree Chakravarti is a healer.
>
> She diagnoses illnesses and cures people through magnetic vibrations of the hand. When her hand passes above a person's body it gravitates towards the troubled spots and pulsates rapidly or slowly in ways that indicate to her the nature of the ailment. While her fingers

register the sensations her whole arm throbs as though filled with an electric current. Doctors who have witnessed her cure, or have taken it themselves as many have, marvel at her extraordinary powers. They acknowledge the efficacy if these powers even though they cannot explain them. They are even beyond those of the conventional faith healer.

When doctors in Germany wanted to study her powers by applying electric cathodes to measure the energy she transmits while curing, she flatly refused fearing she would lose her powers. To her they are a gift of God which she must revere and use to help her fellow human beings. These have included in addition to medical men, high government officials, heads to foreign missions, those in modest walks of life, and children. She has cured them of kidney ailments, heart problems, meningitis, and various forms of paralyzing diseases. She never has and never will accept payment.

She visited Saudi Arabia in 1972. Here she treated the most exalted and the humble alike. She says in God's eyes there are no distinctions between people and she makes none in doing her work. She was warmly welcomed here in Arabia where healers have been known for millennia. Moveover, it has been a profession studded with the names of women, one of the foremost having been Hafsa, a wife of the Prophet Muhammad, renowned for healing powers and knowledge of herbal medicine.

Although she treats a range of ailments, Sree Chakravarti is especially concerned with kidney problems. She is acutely aware of the key role the kidneys play in good health. While she administers her cure through hand vibrations she also prescribes simple treatments such as drinking water in which *kulthi* (dolichos biforus) has been soaked to help cleanse the system. She stresses the importance of drinking good water reminding one that in countries with oil, the water is full of minerals that are bad for the kidneys. When she was in Saudi Arabia she noted a high incidence of kidney disorders. Along with plenty of purified water she mentioned that watermelons and cucumbers also act as good cleansing agents. Coffee, however, she said, if taken at all should be consumed in modest amounts adding that the Arabs have the wise habit of serving coffee with water.

Sree Chakravarti's reputation had spread far and wide. People have come from abroad especially to receive her cure while she has also been invited to attend people in many countries besides Saudi Arabia including Lebanon, Egypt, Kuwait, Iran, Germany, and Canada. Sree has hosts of letters of gratitude from people she has cured.

To those of the nuclear age brought up in the traditions of modern science, what cannot be explained or demonstrated is often dismissed or suspect. Yet those who come close to the extraordinary by witnessing it or experiencing it are often catapulted into a belief and reverence for that which eludes explanation. Such is the impact of Sree Chakravarti.

As I sat in the room where she attends people, a man appearing to be in his forties arrived for treatment. He had had open heart surgery. After complications set in, he began going to this gifted woman while continuing to see his own doctor. Very soon, both he and his doctors noted his marked improvement at the hands of Sree Chakravarti.

He is a modern man. He completed his studies in New York and is at the top of his profession. As Sree's hand vibrated above him we fell into talk about our university studies, work, and his cure. When I asked him. "Do you believe?' he answered without a moment's hesitation, "Yes, I believe."

15

AN INOPERABLE BRAIN TUMOR AND OTHER UNUSUAL CASES

I am often asked to treat unusual cases, many times because the doctors have been unable to diagnose or cure them. Frequently I have no idea if I can help until I try. I know from experience that I am not successful in some areas, or that treating certain problems drains too much of my energy now that I am older, but I can still be surprised to discover what my hand's vibrations will heal. It also seems to be true that my powers are increasing all the time.

An Inoperable Brain Tumor

Almost as soon as I returned to India from Saudi Arabia I began to treat a very difficult case — a young girl whose brain tumor was inoperable because it was inside a blood vessel. She was in her last year of medical studies and had such dreadful headaches she could not sleep or keep up with her class work. She was a pitiful sight with her left eye closed, her mouth pulled down on the left side, and with little strength in her left arm or leg.

My hand located the tumor in her head and I knew if it had taken a long time to grow, it would take a long time to dissolve. When I started her treatment, my hand would vibrate for more than an hour. She came to me every day and eventually this hard work paid dividends. Slowly the headaches disappeared and she could sleep, but she was afraid she would not be allowed to sit for her final exams as she'd had to miss so many classes.

One of our government ministers was coming to me for treatment at the time. Through his friendship with a leading doctor, my patient was allowed to continue her studies and, after a full year of treatment, she passed her M.B.B.S.. She later passed her M.D. and was able to marry and lead a normal life. This was one of my hardest cases.

Leaking Brain Fluid

During the same period I was asked to treat a young woman whose brain fluid ran from her nose unless she kept her head up at all times. Even to drink a cup of tea was almost impossible for her. Her husband begged me to see his young wife. "The doctors want to operate, but they warn us it is a very dangerous procedure. Won't you please see if you can help."

On her first visit, I found the whole skull was soft, like a newborn baby's. Even her cheekbones were very tender and soft. She told me she could not comb her hair properly and could wash it only with great difficulty. My hand vibrated on her whole head, then it started moving towards her forehead. Suddenly I noticed a small scar there. I was sure it was the root of the problem and asked her to tell me about this scar.

"When I was very young I hit my forehead on the iron window grill," she said. "It raised a permanent lump. When I married, my brother-in-law, who is a surgeon, told me I'd look much prettier without the lump. He said it would only be a minor operation under a local anaesthetic." She went on to tell me that in the process of removing the lump he'd exposed her brain by mistake, and had then quickly stitched the wound closed without telling her what had happened.

"Some months later I was cooking for a big festival at home. I tried to lift a heavy pan from the oven, and I felt as if something burst inside my head. Some fluid started flowing from my nose. I thought I'd just got a sudden, violent cold, but the fluid tasted funny." She'd been rushed to a doctor and the liquid was analyzed as brain fluid. The poor young woman had run a constant temperature since and slept with towels around her head to try to stop the flow during the night.

I began treating her three times a week. First her temperature disappeared, then the fluid started to flow less and less. After six months it stopped altogether and the patient made a slow but total recovery.

"My Leg Is on Fire"

One patient came to me most unwillingly as he did not believe in spiritual healers. But the doctors had not been able to help him and he was in such agony he was prepared to try anything. He described to me the nerve problem in his leg. "My whole leg feels as if it is on fire. Even in this freezing cold Delhi winter I cannot bear to cover it." In the hospital, painkillers were all the help doctors could offer him.

When I first examined the man, I was puzzled. My hand did not vibrate at all on the bad leg. "You haven't any problem in this leg," I told him.

"I was testing you," he confessed.

My hand fairly danced on the bad leg. "I just can't believe you can really diagnose my problem with your hand," he exclaimed. "This is something really supernatural." With my touch and the vibration he immediately felt great relief. That night he slept without painkillers and after only a few sittings, he became completely well.

The only problem was he was so excited about being cured he wanted to tell everyone he met about me and how lucky he was to be healed. As a result I got too many people ringing me up. "I just cannot attend to all these cases," I told him, but he paid no attention. I remember he sent me one elderly man who could not stand straight due to some problem with his spine. "How long have you had the problem?" I asked him. He named a year before I was born. "If you've lived with your problem since before I was born," I said, "I'm sure you can live with it for the rest of your life!"

Two Wounds That Would Not Heal

About this time I was asked to treat an army officer who had been thrown from a car in an accident. He had been hospitalized and unconscious for several days, and since regaining consciousness he had suffered severe headaches. In his right temple, he had a small hole from which thick pus oozed out. The doctors were unable to clear it up.

When I examined him, my hand didn't vibrate on the temple where he had the hole, but on the top of his head. I could feel the wound was very deep down and I was sure that this deep wound was the source of the infection. During my treatments, the discharge became thinner and the color pinkish and the headaches stopped. Finally, the doctors were able to stitch the hole closed and the officer recovered completely.

Another army officer, a lieutenant-colonel, had a similar problem with a wound that would not heal. He had had a major operation on his esophagus at the military hospital in Pune. The scar ran from the front to the back of his body, but there was also a small hole about six inches below his armpit from which thick pus was coming. "I was all right for some time after the original surgery," he told me, "then one day this hole appeared. I went back to the hospital and they cleaned and stitched this hole closed, but now it's appeared again. It doesn't hurt me, but it's very worrying."

When I ran my hand down his body, it vibrated on his chest, not over the hole, so I started to treat his chest where he'd had the problem before his surgery. After three sittings with me, while his wife was changing his bandage, thirty pieces of silk thread and three to four stitches came out. After that the pus stopped and my hand no longer vibrated.

The lieutenant-colonel came to thank me, but he was so choked with emotion he could not say what he wanted to. He was actually crying as he seized my hand and kissed it. I was uncomfortable to see such a high-ranking officer in tears, so I told him. "Please, is not me you should thank. It is God's grace that you are cured and you should be grateful to Him. I am only the instrument of His hand."

Headaches and Tragedy

One of my strangest and saddest cases was a woman journalist with severe headaches. She begged me to take her as the painkillers the doctors had given her didn't help. When I first touched her head I could feel she was suffering from extreme tension. She told me she was relaxed and without pain after seeing me. I took an immediate liking to her and one day she confided to me the sad story of her life.

She had married an eminent doctor in an arranged marriage. After two years she had given birth to a pretty daughter, but without any apparent reason, her headaches had started. Her husband did nothing to help her. She sought medical aid, but her headaches only got worse.

She again became pregnant and this time her husband was determined to have a son. He forced special hormones on her daily, even though she protested and tried to vomit them up. When the second child was a girl, he said it was all her fault and virtually deserted the home. Her headaches were by now unbearable.

In despair, she went to a psychiatrist and told him about her marriage. "I believe your husband is impotent," he said, "if you have made love so seldom." When she protested she had become pregnant twice, he said her husband had probably taken powerful medicines to make him temporarily normal. In the psychiatrist's opinion, her headaches were caused by the abnormal relationship.

When she confronted her husband with this diagnosis, he was furious. He accused her of being a loose woman and deserted her for a mistress. But the real tragedy was the second child. Due to the hormones forced on her mother during pregnancy, the child was more like a boy than a girl, with broad shoulders and narrow hips, tiny breasts and an improperly formed uterus. To make problems worse, her pretty older sister made fun of her "for behaving like a boy." When I met the girl she told me she was not interested in clothes or jewelry and felt happiest in the company of boys, she had nothing in common with girls her own age. In spite of all these problems, she was a gifted artist with a lovely nature.

I wish her story had a happy ending. The girl got a scholarship to study art in Paris where she fell in love. After her marriage, she discovered her husband was impotent. She knew her mother's sad story and she committed suicide. I can never forget that beautiful girl — she was like a flower bud that was never allowed to blossom.

A Knee Damaged by Machine-Gun Fire

I have many army patients as one officer sends another to me. I remember an army brigadier whose knee had been damaged by machine-gun fire. Even after an operation his knee would not bend at all and he was in constant pain. On his first visit, he had to have two friends help him up the stairs, but after my initial treatment, he was able to walk down the stairs alone. After a few sittings, he became completely cured.

He had only to put a little leather padding in one shoe as the bad leg was fractionally shorter than the other. He became a major-general and has sent many patients to me over the years.

Two Unusual Headache Cases: Heavy Pots and Hair Dye

One of the first cases this major general sent me was an officer's wife with severe headaches centered on the top of her head. Her doctors had done all the tests, but could find no cause. When I put my hand on her head, it started to vibrate more on the very top and I found a depression there that was extremely tender.

"Have you ever carried anything heavy on your head?" I asked her. It wasn't the sort of question you'd normally ask an army officer's wife. Village women daily carry heavy loads on their heads as a matter of course, but not a woman of this class.

"How strange it is you are asking, but I have been carrying water quite recently," she told me. "My husband was posted on active duty and I went to be with his family. It's only a small village, and they have to bring drinking water for the house. They have no servant to do it, so all the ladies are bringing the water from this well far away. I have never done such work before. Do you think it could have injured my head?" I was sure this was the cause and after several treatments the depression in her head disappeared and her headaches ceased.

Another woman came to me with such severe headaches, she couldn't bear to read or sew, or use her eyes in any way. When she got one of these headaches, she had to sit with her eyes closed but, even so, she would see painful light.

I found my hand did not vibrate over her eyes at all, but over one particular nerve in her head. I remembered reading an article about how certain hair dyes can cause problems. "Do you use dye to blacken your hair?" I asked.

"I think you are right, my headaches did start after I began dying my hair," she exclaimed, "and they always start just in that place where your hand vibrates." She changed to a different dye and after a few sittings, her headaches disappeared and her sight problems ceased.

A Mistaken Diagnosis

I remember another brain tumor case. A young woman was lying unconscious at the All India Institute of Medical Science, perhaps due to an overdose of dye after an angiogram test. "Please come and help her," her husband begged me, "the doctors have said they can do nothing."

My hand vibrated all over her head, but I could not locate the tumor because she had so much dye in her body. On my third sitting she was conscious, and I was able to find the tumor just above the right ear and to tell her husband the size. "But the doctors have said the tumor is in the front of her head," he told me.

The surgeon operated within the next few days and opened her skull above the forehead. They found nothing there. Then they opened the skull where I had said it was and found the tumor. Her husband was very angry with the doctors. "Mrs. Chakravarti found the tumor in only a few minutes and she was correct. You gave my wife so much dye she became unconscious, and your diagnosis was wrong."

After surgery, the woman's wound would not heal and again I was called in. I found her right side was paralyzed and she could not talk. I remember her looking at me and playing with the gold chain around my neck. I went for several days and she improved very fast. I left in her in that condition, when again her husband came for my help. During a test to check her brain fluid, the doctors had used an infected needle and she had got tuberculosis. This time I said I could not help because I cannot cure that sort of infection. Every time, due to their negligence, the doctors made her ill again. I feel very sad that I never heard what happened to her in the end.

Called in to Help a Famous Doctor

I was called in to treat another case of a fast-growing tumor. This time the patient was a very famous doctor from Kanpur. His two brothers, who asked me to help, told me how the doctor had gone for a walk and, on his return, had sat down to read the newspaper. He suddenly got a severe headache, could not see, and felt he was going to faint. "Get a test done on my head," he'd said to his wife before he passed out. When they operated in the Delhi hospital, the tumor was found to be malignant. When I visited the hospital, I asked the nurse to give him some painkiller. "But he's sleeping," she protested.

"Yes, and he's groaning with pain in his sleep," I told her. After the injection he was peaceful. "I believe the tumor has grown again," I said to his brothers. "If I try to treat your brother, the doctors will say my vibrations have caused the problem. It is my instinct he will not survive more than five to six days at the most." The patient died two days later.

Sinus Giddiness

While my work is by no means accepted by every doctor in New Delhi, a certain number of doctors have sought me out for diagnosis and treatment for themselves, their patients and friends, and other doctors.

One day a pathologist friend brought a doctor to me for back treatment as I'd cleared up the pathologist's own back problem some time before. I was able to treat his doctor friend, but I was troubled by the way the pathologist himself walked — as if he were drunk.

"I have a tiny tumor, just behind my ear," the pathologist told me. It makes me feel giddy and I can't keep my balance." He told me that he was scheduled to be operated on soon by an ear, nose, and throat surgeon, not an easy operation so near the brain.

I remembered when the pathologist first came to me for his own slipped-disc problem, I'd also treated him for sinus. "Have you had any sinus attacks recently?" I asked.

"I had a severe attack a short time ago. I had to take antibiotics and it was after that this balance problem started."

"Please let me examine you when I've treated your friend," I said. I found the phlegm of the sinus had hardened — it was not a tumor at all. After the first few sittings he already felt better. The vibrations dissolved the phlegm and no surgery was necessary.

A Case of Typhus

This pathologist next asked me to treat his daughter. She had been running a temperature for over a month, they had done all the tests, but nothing was detected. My hand vibrated only on the girl's lymph glands and on the thymus gland. I felt helpless to treat her, but next day her mother telephoned to say the girl's temperature had come down and to beg me to continue.

After three to four sittings, the girl complained of stomach ache. They thought perhaps she could not digest fried food, but when her father again tested her blood, they found typhus. It seems the vibrations had made it possible to detect the source of the infection. The girl had only been given aspirin, which should not be given in cases of typhoid fever.

"I Can't Stop Crying"

A recent very strange case was that of an Indian lady who had not been able to stop weeping for nearly eight years. She had gone to doctors in London and New York without success. "Strangers are always coming up to me and asking if they can help me," she told me, "they think I have some terrible sorrow."

I told her I'd never even heard of a case like hers, but my hand vibrated near her eyes and even on the first sitting, the flow was less. She was so excited, she was smiling and smiling. She came to me for several weeks and was able to return to London more or less normal. Several months later, her husband came to Delhi from London and telephoned me to say his wife's tears had not resumed and how grateful he was to me. I have also treated two cases of the reverse condition — patients who suffered from eyes that were too dry. I remember in one of the cases, my hand became wet with tears on the first treatment.

Thyroid Gland Problems

Thyroid problems encompass over-active thyroids (hyperthyroidism), and under-active thyroids (hypothyroidism). An over-active thyroid shows up in an enlarged thyroid gland, an increased metabolic rate, a rapid heart beat and rapid weight loss. An under-active thyroid, by contrast, shows up in a general loss of vigor, a lowered metabolic rate, and weight gain.

For some reason, my hand's vibrations can help cure an over-active thyroid, but my treatment does not effect a permanent cure for those suffering from an under-active thyroid. Initially, my hand's vibrations help a patient with an under-active thyroid, but once my treatment stops, the patient's problems resume almost immediately. The only help I can provide for these cases is to tell the patient to practice the *prana mudra*, a yoga finger posture described in Part 2, Chapter 26, and a breathing exercise (funnel breathing) done with the tongue protruding, described in Part 2, Chapter 24. These simple exercises were particularly effective for a young woman I met on one of my trips to Germany. When I first met her she was gaining weight and her throat was so swollen she was slowly losing her voice. I told her I had no time then to help her, but until my return to Munich, to practice the *prana mudra* every day for forty-five minutes. "It will help balance all the elements in your body," I told her.

When I next saw her, about a month later, she was much thinner, and her throat was normal. "This is wonderful, what have your been doing?" I asked.

"I've been doing the *prana mudra* five days a week, twice a day for one hour, on my commute to and from work," she told me. I had never before had such dramatic results with this *mudra* for an under-active thyroid, but I have recommended it very strongly ever since for hypothyroidism and also for many other serious health problems.

I remember when I first discovered that I could help patients suffering from over-activity of the thyroid gland. It was one year during the month of July, when I normally do not work due to the intensely hot weather in Delhi. A friend's wife came to me suffering from hyper-thyroidism. In spite of the medicine the doctors had prescribed, she was losing weight rapidly, she was feeling very weak, her hair was beginning to fall out, and her fingers were stiffening. "I've never treated such a case before," I told her, "but I will try." After several treatments from my hand she appeared cured. This was confirmed by doctor's tests when she returned home to Bombay.

Another patient who came to me was an army general with weight loss problems. He had been tested for everything but thyroid. The doctors had seen a shadow in the lower part of his abdomen on the X-ray, but the army doctors and the doctors at the All India Institute of Medical Science could not agree and would not cooperate on the case.

When I checked the general, my hand vibrated mildly on his liver, but became very active on his thyroid. It happened that a doctor was waiting to ask me to give an appointment to one of his patients. He was interested to know how I diagnosed the case. I told him I judged it was over-activity of the thyroid. The doctor got very interested and wanted to check the general himself. He asked the general to stretch out his arms, and pointed out how his fingers trembled slightly, a common symptom of hyperthyroidism. "This confirms Mrs. Chakravarti's diagnosis," he said. After several treatments from me, the general's weight stabilized and he gradually made a total recovery.

After this case, several doctors from the All India Institute of Medical Science came to see me. They wanted to investigate the phenomenon of cures by studying my hand's vibrations. I could not take part in their experiment as I had accepted an invitation to visit Teheran. While in Iran, I was told by doctors there that I should never expose myself to any type of electrical investigation as it might damage the fine electrical impulses that pass through my fingers.

Thyroid Misdiagnosed as Parkinsons

A strange case involved a man who came to me having been diagnosed as suffering from Parkinson's disease. He was losing weight very fast, he was very weak and he was not improving under medical treatment. On his first visit, he wasn't strong enough to climb the stairs and I came down to check him while he lay in the car. I found my hand vibrated over his thyroid and I asked if he had been tested for problems there. "No, but please treat me for whatever you think is wrong with me," he said.

He was carried upstairs for the first two sittings, but after the second treatment he was able to walk downstairs by himself. He stopped losing weight and started to feel hungry. His liver was also affected and this began to heal. By the time I finished treating him, he was eating and sleeping normally. On top of that, his hands stopped shaking. Apparently, the diagnosis of Parkinson's was a mistake.

Treating a Bad Burn

One of my first burn cases came when I was asked to treat a child who'd been badly burned when her nylon frock caught fire. The little girl was in the hospital, her wounds were not healing, and she was screaming with pain.

"I'm afraid I will have to touch her for my treatment to work," I told her parents. The poor child cried out when I first put my hand on her, but she stopped after a few minutes and I was able to work in peace. The next time I went to treat her, she was so happy to see me. Her mother told me she had gone for a whole twelve hours without pain. After my treatments, her condition improved very fast.

The day came when I told them she was now healed and my work was finished. The child was so upset to think she would not see me again, she would not talk to me or say goodbye.

Treating Brain Damage

I usually do not take patients without an appointment, but I could not refuse the young jet pilot, a squadron leader in the Indian Air Force, who knocked on my door. He had come from Bangalore on the chance I'd see him. He had been grounded after a motorcycle accident had damaged his brain. "The doctors call it atrophy of the brain and say they can't help me," he said. "One day I heard someone talking about you at the Bangalore airport, so I came immediately to Delhi and took a chance I'd be able to find you." When I put my hand on his head, it started to vibrate on one very small spot and I could feel the vibrations going very deep down.

"Can you feel the vibration?" I asked him.

"It feels as if something is piercing right through my head," he said. After a few sittings, the vibrations stopped. When he went back for a check-up, there was no sign of brain damage and he was able to fly again. This pilot sent another pilot to me. This young man had fainted during a flight. He had come to when the plane had gone into a steep dive, but he'd been grounded. I was able to cure him, and both pilots begged me to give an interview to the newspapers so that I would be able to help others like them.

"I am much too busy," I said. "I cannot work more than I do, and I always try to avoid publicity."

Another pilot came to me to be treated for agonizingly painful headaches. None of the doctors he'd seen had been able to help. My hand found a lump near the base of his head, it felt like a nodule of bundled nerves. As I worked, the pain lessened and the nodule disappeared.

I met this pilot many years later and he told me he had never felt the headache or acute pain again. He told his doctor about me and this doctor sent me many patients.

A Hairline Crack in the Skull

Another patient with severe headaches was the son of a government minister. At Chandigarth Hospital, where the father knew everyone, the diagnosis was that the young man suffered from too much blood and should have blood drawn from time to time. Whenever this was done, his wife told me he couldn't stand any noise — he'd start to scream if he heard a car outside, or a curtain was pulled.

When I checked him, I found a hairline crack in his skull. "Have you fallen at any time?" I asked. At first he said no, but when I pressed him, he remembered falling off a sofa while sleeping. I treated him for the hairline crack and, after the first sitting, he felt so well he told me he must be cured. I told him he must come several times in order to become truly healed. After the treatments were finished, he got an assignment abroad and I didn't see him anymore. However, his father told me his headaches had never recurred.

Unexplained Seizures

Another man I treated was a former airline pilot who'd been grounded for unexplained seizures. The attacks would be so violent the doctors would have to inject special sedatives. He had been to London and been told by the English doctors he had "some problem in his head." He was given medicines, but nothing helped him to control the attacks.

When I checked, I found there was nothing wrong with his head, but that my hand vibrated on his neck, just below the ear. The minute I touched the spot, he went into convulsions. "Send for the doctor," his wife screamed. I quickly checked his foot for the pressure point affected. I massaged the area on his foot where my hand vibrated, and brought him back to normal very quickly.

He told me he always knew when the attacks would happen. "Massage your foot at this special point when you feel an attack coming on and you should be able to prevent it," I told him. From that time, he has never had another attack. He was only very sad he did not hear of me before, he had suffered for many years before he met me.

Foot Reflexology

I should explain here that I discovered early in my healing that my hand vibrates on the nerve terminal in the foot that corresponds to the problem area in the body. Although foot reflexology is well understood and widely practiced in India, I have never actually had to study the physiology and pressure points of the foot. In fact, it wasn't until I was on a visit to Germany and one of my friends there gave me a book on foot reflexology that I realized I had been practicing it all along. Whenever it is appropriate, I recommend it to my patients for them to use in helping cure themselves of a wide range of problems from bursitis to weaknesses of the heart.

16
VISITS TO MAURITIUS, IRAN, AND KUWAIT

For several years after my visit to Saudi Arabia, I stayed in India, busy with my healing work. When I started traveling again, I went first to Mauritius, a tiny island in the Indian Ocean near Madagascar. I was invited by the chief minister and I was particularly happy to accept because, for the first time, my husband agreed to accompany me.

From the air, Mauritius looks like a small dot in the ocean, and the pilot had to make two attempts before he could land. The whole island is like a picture postcard, every house has a beautiful garden full of roses and other flowers. Even though the island is so small, you can find extremes of weather. Up in the strangely shaped volcanic mountains it can be quite cold, while on the coast it is warm and humid.

Most of the people now living in Mauritius originally came from India to work as laborers in the sugar cane fields, although several of the people I met insisted on their superior social status because their ancestors had come to do business. I found all of them very kind, generous, and simple, with a religious tolerance I wish the whole world could learn. They celebrate each other's religious festivals and do not make religion an issue when they marry. It is a common thing to see a household where the daughter is Hindu while one daughter-in-law is Muslim, and another Christian.

The chief minister gave a large reception for us the day after we arrived, and he was very keen for me to give an interview on television about my healing. "I will be glad to give the interview, but you must not allow it to be shown before I leave, otherwise it will be too difficult to control all the people who will come," I told him. I was also interviewed by the local paper, and I remember the photographer was so interested when I demonstrated my healing that he forgot to take the picture! Everyone wanted to meet my husband, and he was asked to make a speech in Hindi about how my hand vibrates.

The only sad thing about our visit was how many of the island's people were unhealthy. I believe part of the problem is that with such a small population, there is a lot of intermarriage. Also, few people believed in physical exercise and almost no one drank water. Children and adults alike all drank large bottles of soft drinks, and the younger generation was also too fond of alcohol. As a result, a lot of young people were suffering from gastric ulcers or kidney failure. It was particularly shocking to see the number of children needing dialysis.

I worked very hard to treat a good number of cases each day, but the day we were to leave Mauritius I saw a frighteningly long queue of people coming to see me. They had shown my interview on television the night before and hundreds of people, rich and poor, had come to seek me out.

I began to treat the first in line, but I realized the situation was getting out of hand. There was already such a crowd of people, more than I could ever treat, and more coming every minute. We had to leave quietly by the back entrance and flew to India that evening. Over the years many patients from Mauritius have come to India to be treated by me, but to my regret I have never been able to accept the many invitations I've had to return.

Visit to Iran

Soon after we arrived back in India, I was invited to spend a month in Teheran, Iran, by Cherry, a close friend I had previously treated in Delhi. Her husband, Yacub, was a mining engineer and at the time his very senior job for the Shah's government had kept him in India. They had told several of their friends about me and the whole group had joined together to sponsor my visit.

I went to Iran when the Shah seemed to be at the height of his power. Iran was like a western country with all the amenities of life — big American and European cars, very modern hotels, large posh houses, restaurants, and cinemas. You saw very few women wearing the long black *burka*. From outside, life looked peaceful and easy. Later I was told that, inside, things had already started going wrong between the Shah and the country's spiritual leaders who distrusted modern ways. The Shah was also too much of a dictator, with a secret police force that killed or imprisoned many of those who opposed him. Not too long after my return to India the Shah was exiled and the whole country came under the rule of the Muslim fundamentalists.

As soon as I arrived in Teheran, I began working out of Cherry and Yacub's house. Cherry and her son arranged all the appointments, took care of the phone, answered the door and so on. Most days we were so busy with patients, Cherry did not have time to cook even a simple meal. I used to worry, but she was very happy as more and more people were treated by me. Even though I worked hard, it was one of my best trips.

One day a pretty teen-age girl arrived in an ambulance and was carried into the house on a stretcher. She had been bedridden for some time and the doctors could not find out what was wrong. One leg was held up in a sling and the sister who accompanied her told me the girl had been unable to lower it for several days, screaming in pain if even a fly landed on her leg or foot.

"Well, I can't work on her if I can't touch her," I said and before she could reply I put my hand on the girl's body and found she had a cramp in her urinary passage. She was unconsciously trying to ease the cramp by pulling up her leg. Slowly I started working on her urinary passage and slowly I pushed my hand behind her back to her kidney area. As I worked, her muscles relaxed and she was able to put down her leg.

"Will I be able to walk again?" she asked. "The doctors told me not to try."

"Of course you will walk," I comforted her. I meant she'd walk after a few treatments, not right away, but when I went to wash my hand, as I always do after treating a patient, her sister told her to try. "If you don't have any pain, see if you can walk. If anything happens to you, the Indian lady will be responsible," I was told the sister had said.

When I came back to the passage where the girl had been lying, I had a real shock. The stretcher was empty and there was no trace of my patient. I was a bit frightened until I saw her outside, walking with a slight limp. She came up to me, very excited, and hugged and kissed me. I told her she must come for several more treatments before she would be cured and gave her a time to return the next day. She went home in the ambulance sitting up, waving and smiling. The ambulance driver told me that if all Indian ladies had this healing power, he would find an Indian girl to marry!

In the meantime, all the other patients who had been waiting to see me got very excited. Without my knowing, one of them slipped away to a local newspaper office. She told them about the young girl and what time she would come the next day for treatment.

When the girl came the next day a journalist was there with a photographer from an Iranian newspaper, the *Kayhan International*. I gave an interview on how I heal, but I asked the reporter not to give Cherry's address. When the interview appeared about the "miraculous" healer the address was included. The phone rang night and day and so many people came to the house, it was impossible to work. Cherry decided to take me to her family's cottage on the Caspian Sea to relax for a few days. When no one could find us at home, they went to the newspaper office. Finally the newspaper had to publish an article saying I'd returned to India as their top people couldn't sleep at night for all the phone calls to their homes. The editors told us they'd never had a problem like this in all their years of publishing.

When we returned from the Caspian Sea to Teheran after a few days, I was invited to meet a number of local doctors. I was warned the doctors would be very critical and challenging. My heart was beating very fast when I went to the luncheon and I told Cherry to stay right beside me. A week or so earlier, I had met an Iranian doctor and cured her husband's spinal problem. It was her intervention that saved me when all the doctors started asking me medical questions I could not answer.

My doctor friend stood up when she could see I was getting upset. "Don't ask her medical questions," she said. "She's explained she doesn't have medical training. Let her show you with her hand how she heals. If any of you have a problem you want diagnosed, lie down on this couch and she will tell you what is wrong with you."

One by one I diagnosed several of the doctors' medical problems, all correctly. Then one of the doctors noticed the rings I always wear on my fingers. "Can you diagnose without your rings?" he challenged me.

I was amazed. "Of course, " I said, "do you want me to take off all my rings, my bracelets, my watch? I'll take them all off. They have nothing to do with my healing." I was truly surprised that a doctor should think you could diagnose or heal with a ring. "Now you have all seen my work, please ask me any questions you like and I will try to reply."

They were all silent. Then one of them spoke up. "We have all heard about healers," he said, "but we have never met one with such quick and accurate powers of diagnosis." They asked me if I would demonstrate my healing to more doctors, but I had to refuse as my time in Teheran was up.

One young Iranian woman who had read about me in the newspaper actually followed me to India. She'd been working in her office when she got a phone call to say her husband had been in a serious car accident. She'd jumped up so quickly to rush out that she'd fallen and hit her head against the wall, leaving her with facial paralysis. As soon as her husband was better, she got my home address from a Teheran newspaper and came to me in Delhi for a successful treatment.

Cherry, and most of the people I met in Teheran, were Muslim. In those days none of us thought about religion. Today I wonder how all those wonderful human qualities of tolerance and friendship have vanished from the face of the earth and, deep down from our unconscious, all the evil qualities like hatred, violence and greed are coming up and like a volcano, spreading the lava of our own destruction.

Visit to Kuwait

About two months after my return from Teheran, a friend returned from Kuwait and told me that a Kuwaiti government minister, Mr. Abdul Aziz, was going to invite me and my husband to their country. He had heard about my healing from my old friend, the former Syrian ambassador to India, Omar Abu Riche. A few days later, we received two first-class return air fares. I was very keen to go, but my husband was upset about me leaving the country again so soon and he was busy with his own affairs. He told me he had no time to go and get permission from the Reserve Bank. I decided to see the bank myself and at first was refused permission to leave the country. I did not give in, and when I asked the bank officials to put their objections in writing, they agreed I could go.

I stayed in Kuwait for about two weeks, treating people in my big modern hotel suite. Many of the cases were very serious — a lot of back problems, gastric and duodenal ulcers and kidney problems. I was able to cure one young boy of asthma with a yoga breathing exercise, the *sasanka asana*, which I describe in Part 2, Chapter 25. One of the most interesting cases was a minister who had severe breathing problems. When I examined him, I found his lungs were not elastic at all. When I asked him about his daily life, he told me he owned an asbestos factory where he went each day. I told him the asbestos particles he inhaled must have cemented his bronchial tubes. I could not heal him in the time I was there and could only advise the same breathing exercise I recommended to the boy with asthma.

Mr. Abdul Aziz was a big businessman as well as a minister, with a contract to build many of the large hotels. He and his wife were very friendly and often invited me to their house for lunch or dinner. Although his wife could not speak English, somehow we became close friends. One day Abdul Aziz told me I'd been invited to accompany him and his wife to a tea party where I would also attend some patients. I could not refuse although I was tired and felt I had no time to go to parties. Our hosts were very rich and, after treating a few patients, I was taken on a long tour of the house. "This is the blue bedroom, this is the pink bedroom, this marble comes from Italy, this vase is from China." I thought the tour would never end. The minister, who was with us, could see I was not at all interested. Finally I cut short the visit, telling them I would be late for my next patient. "I'm afraid you did not enjoy your visit" Abdul Aziz asked as we drove back to my hotel.

"I have come here to attend patients, not to see a display of wealth," I told him. "In future, I will not visit anyone here, whoever they are."

"I never thought they would behave like that, I am truly sorry," Abdul Aziz apologized. "But then I have never met anyone before like you who has so little interest in the material world." I was asked to stay on to treat more patients, but I felt I must get back to my husband and to my responsibilities in India.

A Visitor from Iraq

After I'd returned from Kuwait, I had a visitor from Iraq who'd read about me in the Kuwaiti newspapers. She brought her child with her, a girl of about two years old, whose wrists were wrapped in cloth to prevent her chewing on the skin. All the time she was there, she was biting on the cloth. Her mother explained the child had begun biting her wrists about a year ago after she'd been severely jolted in a car when they'd had to stop very abruptly to avoid hitting a pedestrian. The parents had taken their daughter to doctors in the United States and England without them being able to diagnose the problem. As the child was only about one year old at the time she was seeing these doctors, they had not wanted to do tests on her brain.

"If it happened over a year ago, I don't know if I can diagnose her problem now," I said, "but let me examine her." My hand vibrated on a particular part of the brain, and the minute my hand started vibrating the child became peaceful and stopped biting on the cloth. Her eyes looked vacant, unfocused. When my hand stopped vibrating, she again began her biting.

"Let her come for a few treatments, and we will see if she improves," I told the mother. After several sitting, the little girl stopped the biting altogether. Her mother told me she had started to be interested in television and to show love for her brother. I felt sure the sharp jolt in the car had injured some portion of the brain. With my treatment she got cured completely. Her mother was so happy for the child that she said good-bye to me with tears in her eyes. Now I not only wonder if they are still well, but also if they all survived the Gulf war.

17

VISITS TO CANADA AND CALIFORNIA

During 1981 I accepted invitations to visit Toronto, Canada, twice, and I went once to California. The Toronto visits were arranged through close friends, Margaret and Jim Beveridge, who lived for a long time in New Delhi, working on various film projects for UNESCO and for Toronto's York University and the Canadian government.

My first visit to Toronto was in the spring of 1981. It was sponsored by the husband of a friend of the Beveridges whose wife had an intestinal obstruction that prevented her from eating anything solid. Her blood count was very low, she was getting weak very rapidly. Her doctors said they were helpless. I try to avoid cancer patients as I am never sure if I am successful, and I was very reluctant to go as I did not even know if my hand would vibrate on her problem. Also, I could only go for twelve days at the most. When I explained all this to her husband, he still wanted me to come.

When I met the lady she reminded me so much of a friend of mine, I felt I had known her all my life and I immediately began to treat her in her home. After three sittings she started to feel hungry and to eat proper food. Her blood count went up and all the doctors were amazed at her progress. I was able to give her ten sittings and she was well enough to come to the airport to wave goodbye to me.

I also treated my patient's daughter, who could not carry a baby past the fourth month. I examined her and found the mouth of the uterus, the cervix, was very weak. After three long treatments she was able to carry her child the whole nine months and have a normal delivery.

While I was in Toronto, I saw briefly two other patients — one had weak eyes whose vision improved with three sittings, and the other was a case of neck cancer. I told the lady with neck cancer I was very sad, but it would be no use to see her only once, which was all the time I had left.

A Second Visit to Toronto

I was invited back to Toronto in the fall of 1981 by a group of friends of the Beveridges. I spent about three weeks there, with my own flat in the Beveridge's house and two of their friends acting as my secretaries and driving me about in their cars.

One of the people I treated was the daughter-in-law of my friend, Jim George, the former High Commissioner for Canada to India. He always says he first became a grandfather thanks to me. I also treated the lady with an eye problem that I had seen twice on my first visit and she improved a great deal. Previously, she had been afraid to go out in the evening because of her poor vision.

Another of my Toronto patients was a famous opera singer who had a very deep but non-malignant tumor of the brain that the doctors could not totally remove. It used to cause her severe headaches and partial blindness. With my treatment she got back her sight and her headaches almost stopped. She was so much better, she was able to give an interview on television, but the producers wouldn't allow her to talk about my healing — they were afraid of objections from doctors.

I also, of course, spent as much time as I could with my first Toronto patient. Now she had some problem with her hip bone which she was afraid was bone cancer. She was a little upset that because I had so many other patients I could not see her every day, so I sent her treated water the days I could not go.

As I mentioned in connection with treating kidney patients, I discovered at some point in my healing, I really don't quite remember when, that when I put my hand in water, the water boils up around my hand and the water then acquires healing properties. Every morning while I was in Toronto, I would plunge my hand into pails of water and the friend helping me would pour it into sterile bottles and send it to various other friends who needed treatment, including my first patient. After my second round of treatments, she lived for two more years.

A Visit to California and the Esalen Institute

I was invited to visit Los Angeles, California, by the same friends, Cherry and Yakub, who'd arranged for me to go to Teheran. This time, Yacub was able to be at home. As before, Cherry filled their house with friends who needed treatment. Cherry never got upset, no matter how many people she had to cook for. While I was staying with them, Dr. Stanislav Grof, M.D., a visiting fellow at the Esalen Institute, heard I was in Los Angeles. Before I'd left India, I had been invited to Bombay to demonstrate my healing at the Seventh International Transpersonal Conference in February 1982. It was to be chaired by Dr. Grof and he was anxious to meet me and see my work beforehand. He wanted to know how many days I could stay at the Esalen Institute and what I would charge for my time. "I can only come for three days, and I never accept money, but you will have to pay for my plane ticket and for my board and lodging," I told him. He was very surprised and pleased to learn I did not charge for healing.

The two-hour drive from the airport to Big Sur along the coast was very beautiful. I liked Dr. Grof and his wife Christina from the first meeting. Christina had a wonderful smile and was immediately very friendly. They asked me to attend a special workshop after lunch, held in a big hall where I was very happy to see a picture of Sai Baba of Shirdi and to learn they also believed in him.

Raising the Serpent Power

Dr. Grof and Christina told me the afternoon workshop was a special one, held to raise the hidden or serpent power, the *kundalini shakti*. Many people associate serpent power only with sexual arousal, but yogic practice recognizes two forms of serpent power, the lower and the higher. The higher is also called the hidden power, and may be drawn on by healers and artists as a source of strength and inspiration.

At the Esalen workshop, each novice was accompanied by a helper. The newcomers were told to lie down on mattresses and loosen their clothing. Christina put on some soft music and the helpers aided their partners to relax. Then they were told to start breathing slowly, then a little faster, and then to take very deep breaths, quite fast. The music suddenly changed to very loud, violent music, which Dr. Grof told me would awaken the *kundalini shakti*. Suddenly a few of the novices started screaming and crying, others were making noises like animals, some became quite violent. Their helpers were giving them water and wiping away their perspiration. Dr. Grof went from one person to another, putting his hand on their abdomens, his palm touching the navel. This went on for about two hours, when everyone became exhausted and more or less normal. They were all told to write about their experiences which would be discussed when they met again that night at eight o'clock.

"What did you think of the workshop?" Dr. Grof asked when everyone had left the hall. I was very honored to be asked my opinion by a doctor and an authority on altered states of consciousness, but I had to say what I felt.

"I can't help wondering if the whole process is unnatural and perhaps harmful to the nervous system, with all those violent reactions and shakings of the body," I told him. Dr. Grof agreed with me and said this was why they only held this workshop twice a week.

That evening we met again in the big hall and listened to the accounts of what people felt they had experienced. I don't remember all of them, but one person said he had seen Jesus, another had seen only light, several felt they had been in a trance. Unfortunately, the projector failed, so we couldn't see the films of previous *kundalini shakti* workshops and we had time on our hands. Suddenly Dr. Grof asked me to tell them about my work. It was an informal gathering, but still it was an international, sophisticated crowd and I felt I was only an ordinary person, not really qualified to speak. Everyone was looking at me expectantly. I thought for a few minutes then I said, "Why don't you just ask me about my healing work, I really don't know how to give a lecture." Everyone was interested and I was asked to demonstrate my healing energy. We all became so involved that three hours passed before we said good-night to each other.

The next morning at breakfast Christina told me how sorry she was to have missed the meeting. She thought they were just going to show films she'd seen many times before. She told me Dr. Grof had said how glad he was to know about my work before the conference in Bombay. He also commented on how different I was from most of the famous healers that had been invited to Esalen over the years, not only because my way of healing was quite different, but because I refused to accept money or gifts for what I did.

When I got to my workshop, which was to be for three hours in one room, I was surprised to see a huge gathering of people who all wanted me to diagnose their problems and give them a short treatment. I calculated quickly that I couldn't spend more than a few minutes with each person and at the end of the three hours I felt totally exhausted. One of the patients told me she had a spinal problem I had not checked. I told her to come for the afternoon session, but she told me she would not be allowed to come as she had only paid for one session. I didn't realize they were charging people to see me, because I never accept any payment for my healing, but I suppose they had to cover the expense of my coming.

When I returned to Los Angeles, Cherry and Yakub wanted to take me sight-seeing, but I was not really interested. It is very difficult to treat people and also enjoy driving around. I prefer to preserve my energy for the sick and not waste it on my own pleasure and, in any case, it was time for me to return to India.

18
MY FIRST
INTERNATIONAL
CONFERENCE

Before I'd met Dr. Grof at the Esalen Institute in California, he had invited me to demonstrate my healing at the 1982 Seventh International Transpersonal Conference in Bombay. Dr. Grof, who was to chair the conference, had originally heard about me from my old friend, Dr. Ajit Mookerjee, an authority on *kundalini shakti* with many books on the subject to his credit. Dr. Mookerjee, who was living and writing in London, had also been invited to lecture at the conference.

I was very nervous about going to a big international conference where many famous speakers would be featured. I had told Dr. Grof about my fears when I was in California. He and his wife Christina came to Delhi ahead of the conference to reassure me and tell me about the arrangements they had made for me.

When I arrived at the airport in Bombay, a young man had been sent to meet me and take me to my hotel. "How did you recognize me?" I asked him.

"Dr. Grof said to look for the little lady with the big *tikka* mark on her forehead," he said. While we were driving into Bombay he asked me all sorts of questions, trying to find out why on earth I'd been invited with so many important people. "Have you ever been to Bombay before? Will you be nervous about staying in a big modern hotel like the Oberoi — I don't suppose you've ever stayed in a place like the Oberoi, have you?"

"Yes, I've been in Bombay several times," I told him, "and, yes, I've stayed in big hotels, but I just stay where they put me. Sometimes it's a hotel, sometimes it's a private house or a guest house."

"How do you know Dr. Grof? " was his next question. When I told him I'd met Dr. Grof in California, he kept quiet, but I could see he was still very puzzled and not at all sure he could believe me.

When we got to the Oberoi Towers Hotel at Narriman Point, I went straight to the hall where the Governor of Bombay was addressing the meeting. In his speech the governor told us that the conference would show how the ancient wisdom of the East and the modern science of the West are coming closer together and joining hands. This is needed, he said, because there is a growing realization that the purely material approach of Western science must be synthesized with a spiritual approach to existence if we are to grow as people and to have a new world order.

When I looked around at the eminent international crowd of some seven hundred people gathered in the hall, and all the reporters with their video cameras, microphones and tape recorders, I began to feel the young man who'd met me at the airport was right. What, indeed, was I doing there? I did not have any knowledge or wisdom to share with these others. I felt better when I saw Christina, who flashed me a smile of welcome, and my old friend Dr. Mookerjee. They told me my workshop would be at 3:30 that afternoon. The Grofs would be holding a press conference at the time, and Dr. Mookerjee would introduce me.

When I arrived at my workshop, the room was packed with distinguished medical doctors, scientists, pyschologists, biologists, anthropologists, and many more. On the stage there was a boy in a wheelchair who had muscular dystrophy. He gave me a letter from Christina asking me to demonstrate my healing on him.

I stood on the stage, feeling very nervous, waiting for Dr. Mookerjee to come to the front and introduce me. Then Dr. Mookerjee stood up at the back of the room. All he said was, "Please open your brochure at page 10 and read about Mrs. Chakravarti." Then he left the room.

There was a rustling of papers as everyone turned to page 10 of their brochures — "Sree Chakravarti: Diagnosis and Healing by Magnetic Vibrations of the Hand." While they were reading about me, I spoke to the young boy and told him I would try to help him as best I could. I had to explain to him that I do not normally treat muscular dystrophy because I know from experience I cannot cure it. While I was talking to the boy, the audience became restless and started to call out. "Please start your lecture. We're here to hear your lecture." I went to the microphone.

"I really don't know why I've been invited to this conference where everyone is supposed to give speeches," I told them. "It says quite clearly in the brochure that this is a demonstration of how I diagnose and heal. I don't make speeches. I will show you how I use my right hand to heal, and this young man I will be treating here on the stage will tell you what he is feeling."

As I began to work on the boy, everyone started to imitate me, shaking their hands and laughing. I was amazed that a group of such eminent people could be so rude. I had to stop my treatment and walk back to the microphone. "Please be quiet," I said. "Give me a few minutes to work on this boy and then you will have the rest of the time to have all the fun with me you want."

They all became quiet and I continued to work on the boy's spine as I know muscular dystrophy affects that area. As I touched the boy, I asked him to explain to the audience how he felt.

"I feel as if my whole body is vibrating with a current, as if she is putting her hands all over my body, not just on my back," he told the audience. "It's as if lightning is going through my body."

"Is there any doctor in the audience with a physical problem I can try to diagnose?" I asked the group when I had finished treating the boy. A lady stood up and introduced herself as a medical doctor. She said she'd had a back injury for some time that prevented her sitting comfortably. I asked her to come to the stage and sit down on a chair and take off her socks and shoes.

I made a quick diagnosis by vibrating my hand on her feet and applying presure to the nerve terminal my hand told me was the seat of the trouble. "My God, I cannot believe this," she said after only a few minutes treatment. "My back already feels so incredibly much better." I find my intuitive knowlege of foot reflexology is very useful at a conference like this when I have to make a quick diagnosis and demonstrate my healing gift.

After I had treated the young boy and the doctor, the whole atmosphere in the workshop changed. Now all those people who'd been making fun of me wanted me to touch as many of them as possible. I think God was there in that room helping me. I touched as many as I could in the time alloted to my workshop, and when it was finished, several people in the crowd went out and told others about me.

Dr. Grof and Christina were very pleased my workshop had been such a success. "I told you you didn't have to be nervous," Dr. Grof teased me. Then he told me they had made time for me to hold a second, unscheduled workshop in a much larger room because so many people who had missed the first one were asking to see my work. The huge room where I held the second workshop was overflowing with people and yet I was able to make quick and accurate diagnoses as before. They even wanted me to give a third workshop, but it was impossible to fit it into the schedule. Such are the ways of God, I thought, that in spite of all my initial nervousness, I became one of the star attractions at the conference!

One of these workshop patients was Harrison Hoblitzelle, an American professor of psychology from Boston, who'd come to my first workshop in a wheelchair. Since arriving in Bombay he'd been stricken with a terrible pain that had been diagnosed as arthritis. The pain was so unbearable he was thinking of leaving the meeting and flying home for treatment. Harrison has sent me a wonderfully lively account of how he remembers our first meeting.

Case History: Harrison Hoblitzelle

I arrived in Bombay for the conference immobilized by a sudden and mysterious health crisis. What rotten luck, I thought. But that very crisis led to the chance encounter with Sree Chakravarti that proved to be a turning point in my life.

Having traveled around India for a month before the conference, I suddenly developed a painful and progressive stiffening of the left hip

joint that threatened my carefully laid plans for an extended visit.
I was alarmed and dismayed at this sudden disability. My spirits sank.
In Bombay, a Western trained doctor had diagnosed the condition as a
"post-dysentery arthritis" for which there was no remedy except anti-
inflammatory medication and extended bed rest. He urged me to return
home without delay. For someone planning a four-month stay in
India plus a trek in Nepal with a sixteen-year-old son, this was bad
news indeed.

In any case, I arrived at the conference barely able to walk.
Confined to my hotel room, the conference passed me by until the
third morning when my wife, in a state of high excitement and
determination, burst into our room with a wheelchair.

"Get up! You have to come right now. There's a healer who is doing
a demonstration. I've just watched her work on a couple of people.
It's really amazing. And she needs subjects. I'll explain everything in
the elevator."

At first I couldn't believe she was serious. From reading the
conference program, I recalled something about a special demonstration
of "healing by means of magnetic vibrations of the hand," but I had
already dismissed it. The idea stretched my credulity to the breaking
point. Nevertheless my wife can be very persuasive, so, to make a long
story short, I soon found myself, still in my pajamas and feeling foolish,
being wheeled into the crowded hotel ballroom. The atmosphere in the
room was electric. The audience, apparently having just witnessed an
amazing transformation in a previous subject, hung on every word as
Sree Chakravarti, the Indian healer, told stories of similar healings. Still
kneeling in the middle of the room under a spotlight, she beckoned us
to her. After brief introductions, she took charge.

"Come. Come. Lie down here," Sree ordered merrily, as I was helped
out of the wheelchair onto the floor in front of her. Reluctant and
skeptical, to put it mildly, I considered myself a less than likely subject
for an improbable healing experiment. Yet, as Sree continued to talk
animatedly to the room full of people, I was struck by the charismatic
presence of this handsome sari-clad Bengali woman, with her flashing
eyes and ready chuckle. What disarmed me right away was her high
spirited, child-like flow of words and laughter. She seemed
extraordinarily alive and she was obviously having a very good time.

As I lay there on my back starting to tell her about my problem, she
silenced me with a gesture and went right to work. With her right hand

vibrating gently, she began to sweep down my body at a height of about six inches. After a few minutes, she announced cheerfully, "Well. There is nothing wrong with your hip." This was too much. I was incredulous — not to say incensed — that this woman should arrive so quickly at her cheerful conclusion that seemed to brand me as a first-class hypochondriac.

"Do you mean to say you think it's all in my head?" I challenged her. Without responding to my question, she merrily ordered me to "turn over, turn over." As I gingerly rolled over onto my stomach and lay there, my spirits sank. How could this woman contradict my own experience and tell me that there was nothing wrong with the hip? This was the one part of my body that was giving me trouble! My skepticism returned in full force.

Lying there on my stomach, I could no longer see what was happening, but people told me later that she continued her aerial scan of my body, and that when her hand passed over the left kidney, it started to flutter wildly.

"What is this? What is this, Harrison? It is the *kidney*," she declared and then went on to announce to everyone else, with a lighthearted wag of her head, that she had located the problem. This was a stunning moment; her hand had come up with a diagnosis that ran counter both to the experience of my body and the best diagnosis of traditional Western medicine.

With her hand now vibrating vigorously, for the first time she touched me — very gently — on the kidney. It was astonishingly tender; I had never had any kidney problems, nor until that moment did I ever know exactly where my kidneys were! In a digression to the audience, she identified habitual dehydration as the great hidden cause of this and many other health problems: "People don't drink enough water!" she declared.

I interrupted to ask her what she could do to help my frozen hip joint. She told me not to worry, that she had already started to work on it. I could feel her fingers vibrating with the vibrato of a virtuoso violinist as she went back and forth over the kidney area. Meanwhile she continued to entertain the audience with her past experiences as a healer.

By this time my mind was in a free-fall; I didn't know what to make of all of this. I thought to myself, "How can she talk to them while she's working on me? She doesn't even seem to be paying attention! Doesn't she want to know anything more about my symptoms? Anyhow, how can she possibly heal me when I'm so incurably skeptical!"

After a few minutes, Sree announced that she would now work on my feet. Although I had no idea what she was doing, or why on earth she was doing it, there was an agonizing moment as her right hand began to vibrate on what I later learned from reflexology was the kidney point on my foot. Meanwhile, her lighthearted banter with the audience continued on every subject but the one at hand.

The next thing I heard was her order, "All right, get up! Get up!" I thought she was *really* crazy. I had hardly moved for days and she's telling me to just stand up and walk! I carefully got to my feet and tried a few very tentative steps. To my astonishment, I found that the pain was nearly gone. Despite a limp, I could actually walk! The problem was about seventy-five percent gone.

The entire process had only taken about fifteen minutes. In that short space of time, I had somehow found myself at the center of a miracle... and I didn't even believe in miracles. What is the mind to make of that? Here was a miracle of diagnosis as well as healing.

My mind was spinning. As a good Western rationalist, I watched my cherished concepts blown out of the water. A stream of impossible questions assailed me: Why me?... How had I deserved this extraordinary good fortune when so many others had greater need?... How did she do it?... How could healing like take place in the face of such solid skepticism as mine?

For the remaining days of the conference, on Sree's orders, I came to her for daily treatments to complete the healing. By the last day, my hip problem had vanished completely; I was fully recovered. But though my body had healed, my mind was still spinning. During those sessions with Sree, I got up the nerve to voice some of my questions. She made short work of them:

"God brought us together, Harrison. He meant for me to heal you and for you to be healed. It is not for you or for me to question this."

"But Sree, how does this healing work? How could this take place with a person like me who doesn't believe in any of this stuff?"

"Thinking, thinking, you are too much thinking!" she scolded. "It doesn't matter what you are thinking or what I am thinking." She motioned to the picture of Sai Baba of Shirdi, the late Indian saint to whom she attributes the healing power, and then she pointed toward the heavens, her eyes flashing.

"It is all His grace. We do not need to understand everything. My hand knows. I am not doing anything. It is all Sai Baba's Grace coming through my hand. His grace is the healing."

After the conference, I was completely free of symptoms. Against all odds, I even went trekking in Nepal on schedule. Over the years, I have returned several times to India and have always gone to see Sree, as have several members of my family who have also come to her for healing.

It has taken years to assimilate all that has opened within me as a result of these encounters with Sree. I have learned a new respect for the wonder and mystery of things. Over time, I began to understand Hamlet's humbling words to his friend: "There are more things in heaven and earth, Horatio, than are dreamt of in your philosophy."

— Harrison Hoblitzelle
Boston, Massachusetts
USA

I treated another very interesting man at the conference, Cecil Burney, who was sent to me for healing by the Grofs. Burney was a Jungian psychologist and a well-known lecturer on transpersonal psychology in the United States and abroad. He was very interested in my healing and made me promise to hold a workshop at the next international transpersonal conference, which he would be chairing in Davos, Switzerland, the following year.

For me, the real high point of the gathering was meeting Mother Teresa, who addressed the conference on the last morning. Dr. Grof introduced me to her and she was very happy to hear that I treated people without charging. For me it was the fulfillment of my life to meet the only human being who is God on this earth. I could not control my tears when she hugged me.

19

FIRST INTERNATIONAL GATHERING ON SHAMANISM AND HEALING

A few weeks after the Seventh International Transpersonal Conference in Bombay, I was asked by Doctor Dieter Sheid to hold a workshop at the First International Gathering on Shamanism and Healing, organized by the Crystal Association for Life Exploration in Munich. It was held in the beautiful mountain region of Alpbach, Austria, from May 29 to June 4, 1982.

This was a much smaller gathering than the one in Bombay although many of the speakers also came from distant lands — among them were Letty Guirnalda, a teacher and healer from the Philippines working with doctors in Germany; Carmen and Jarbas Marinho, mediums and healers from Brazil; Rolling Thunder, a medicine man from the Cherokee Indian tribe in the United States; Michael Harner, an anthropologist from the New School for Social Research in New York and, in particular, Don Jose Matsuwa, a Huichol Indian shaman from Mexico, on his first visit to Europe. Don Jose was 102 years old at the time of the gathering and an altogether amazing and wonderful man. Because there were comparatively few of us, and a much smaller attendance, it was more like a family meeting than a big conference.

As I understand it, a shaman is a priest-doctor who uses magic to cure the sick and to control forces that affect his people, like asking for rain. Shamanism isn't really a formal religion, but more an expression of loving care for the whole community and the environment.

At the opening of the conference, Dr. Dieter Scheid, who was one of its chief organizers, told us he'd found out it was illegal in Austria to do spiritual healing. He apologized for not knowing this when they had chosen Alpbach for their gathering on shamanism, and he cautioned us not to give interviews to journalists or encourage any publicity. I told Dieter I was very shocked to hear this. "I've found from experience it is almost impossible to keep my healing gift a secret, wherever I go, however hard I try," I had to tell him.

It was arranged I should give two sessions each day to demonstrate my healing. From the first session, I had a good crowd of people and at each session more and more people came, all wanting me to demonstrate my healing on them. As I had more time than in Bombay, I was able to teach them healing yoga postures and how to meditate.

For myself, I was particularly interested in Michael Harner's workshop that I had not had time to go to at the transpersonal conference in Bombay. His aim was to arouse the source of primal energy, or altered state of consciousness, through special breathing techniques and drum beating, following customs he had studied among tribal peoples in North and South America.

I tried my best to do everything we were supposed to do, but I could not feel any of the sensations the others described. I thought perhaps I had not concentrated properly the first time. The second time I joined hands with the others to experience the flow of primal energy, but again I did not experience any of the feelings the others were describing, such as entering a hidden world. I was badly disappointed, but Michael Harner explained I could not have these experiences as I was "different" from normal people.

"You mean it's because I am Indian?" I asked him. "No, it's not because you are Indian — I used the same technique very successfully with many Indian participants at the Bombay conference. It's because you have your own psychic powers," he told me.

One day I had to help the healer from Brazil, Jarbas Marinho. He had a very bad sore throat and in his workshop he had to show a video and then explain it to the participants. "Why don't you ask your wife to heal you?" I said. He told me she had tried, but it had not helped. With one touch of my hand he got his voice back. He was so grateful, he gave me a bracelet made of Brazilian stones.

The second healing I did was on a rabbit! It was a baby rabbit and had fainted with shock when it came onto the road and a car passed by very quickly. Someone picked it up from the roadside and brought it to me. At first the baby rabbit seemed to be cold and lifeless, then my hand started vibrating over its heart and after a few minutes the pulse rate increased and it became warmer. It started taking deep breaths. Everyone was watching and someone took a picture. The tiny rabbit slept on my lap for a few minutes, then suddenly it jumped off and ran away. I like to think it found its way back to its mother.

I thought I could probably cure the rabbit because I had successfully healed our own and two neighbors' dogs. One time I came home and found my husband in great distress with our little Pomeranian lying in a coma at his feet. He told me the dog had been playing happily on our terrace and then had suddenly fallen over. When I ran my hand over our pet it vibrated on her head and I found she had been stung on her nose by a bee. Within a few minutes, the swelling came down and she recovered. I also helped cure two neighbors' dogs — one had been poisoned and the other badly wounded in a dog fight.

The Alpbach gathering was in its third day when the organizers learned that one of the lecturers could not get his visa and they had to find someone to take his place. Dieter put my name up on the hotel board as the speech giver. "I don't give speeches," I begged him, but he wouldn't pay any attention. Then I remembered how I'd managed at the Esalen Institute. "Well, I'll stand there and let people ask me questions if you like, but I simply can't give a proper speech," I finally agreed.

When I got to the auditorium, it seemed like a huge crowd. I started praying silently to Sai Baba. "You must be with me, you must help me," I told him. "If I am disgraced, it is your fault, and if I am honored, it is your honor." Somehow, after that, from inside I got some confidence and when Dieter asked me to first tell them a little about how I became a healer, I found I could speak quite easily and for a much longer time than I had thought possible. I finished by answering a lot of questions. My speech and the questions and answers were all taped. To my surprise, a lot of people bought the cassette to take home with them.

When I'd finished speaking, the first person to congratulate me was Letty. "Oh, Sree, you spoke so well. Let us have lunch together," she said. I was very pleased as I had wanted to be friends with her and I had not felt she liked me. After this we became very good friends.

Dieter asked me why I'd made such a fuss about speaking. "You spoke so well, why is it you wouldn't agree to speak in the first place?" he asked me.

"I told Sai Baba of Shirdi he must take charge," I told them, "he is the Indian saint who is my guide."

"We also trust in God," Dieter told me.

"Then you must leave the steering wheel completely in His hands," I told them.

On Sunday night at dinner I got into trouble with Dieter, but it was not my fault. Countess Keyserling, the wife of the Austrian honorary chairman, asked me to help a young girl on the hotel staff who had a terrible toothache. As it was a Sunday, no dentist was available. The young woman acting as my secretary said I was not allowed to heal anyone unless Dieter agreed. The countess went to his table and they argued for some time. I could see he was angry, but he gave his permission as long as the countess told no one about it.

I treated the girl until she told me she felt much better. Unfortunately, next day she told several people in the little village. Of course, I am rather easy to recognize in my sari and with the big *tikka* mark on my forehead, and when I went out next day with my secretary, Nancy, everyone started coming out of their houses to see me. In no time we were surrounded, and they were all asking me questions in German. Nancy told me they were all wanted to be treated. "Tell them they have made a mistake," I told her.

"I can't, there was an article last week in the local paper describing you and now that girl has told them how you cured her toothache last night." When I heard that, we had no alternative but to go quickly back to the hotel, followed by all the people. I went into the hotel and shut myself in a bathroom. Dieter had to explain to the crowd that I was not allowed to treat them and he was very upset.

One of the healers, whose name I have forgotten, joined the gathering, dressed only in a tiger skin, no shoes, no jacket, and with long flowing hair. He told me he had had to kill the tiger whose skin he wore with his bare hands before he could call himself a shaman. He looked so young and handsome, I could not believe he had grandchildren. A young couple attending the conference wanted this healer to act as a priest and "marry" them and they asked me to be the chief guest. The ceremony was to take place at dawn, with the altar a stone decorated with wildflowers in the middle of a small waterfall. Several of us climbed to the place to find the couple facing the rising sun and the "priest" uttering some strange sounds none of us could understand. The healer had tied the young couple's hands together with a creeper and at the end of the ceremony he told them to walk back down through the flowing water, not by the path we had all used.

"Why are they to do that?" I asked. I was concerned that tied together they would fall and hurt themselves on the slippery rocks.   "The climb down through the rushing waterfall symbolizes the need to hold each other close when one goes through a difficult time in one's married life," was his answer.

When they were safely down, I was asked to bless them. I was at a loss as to what I should give them for a present, then I suddenly remembered the bracelet from Brazil in my purse. That was my wedding gift, and I've often wondered if the young couple are still together.

On the last day of the conference, Dieter and Bat-ya, one of the conference co-organizers, asked me to stay with them in Munich. Bat-ya drove me there and to my great pleasure, Don Jose Matsuwa was also in Munich with his interpreter Brant Secunda. The five of us all celebrated the night of the full moon together. To spend time with Don Jose, such an intensely spiritual man, was one of the experiences of a lifetime that I will always cherish. He reminded me of the eagle in the poem, "Song of the Journey," by Josie Tamarin:

> *Life stirs*
> *Light stirs us all*
> *And an eagle soars towards the sun*
> *On the sighs of our awakening.*

20
VISIT TO LONDON

Dr. Mookerjee, who had been responsible for my being invited to the Seventh International Transpersonal Conference in Bombay, now asked me to come to London during the late summer of 1982 to treat a number of patients he'd arranged to have sponsor me. I was to stay in his house and treat the people there. Unknown to me and to him, one of sponsors, Rory, had a serious case of cancer. Dr. Mookerjee apologized when I'd talked to Rory on the phone. He knew I avoided cancer patients because they drain too much of my health and strength and because I am never sure I can really cure them.

"Rory's wife is Austrian, from Alpbach, and she had heard all about you," he told me. "When I mentioned you were coming, her husband immediately offered to pay most of your fare. I'm sorry I didn't find out exactly what was wrong with him, but please go and see him. He is in severe pain and it will be very hard for him to come here to see you."

When we got to Rory's house, we found he was alone there with his housekeeper — his wife was at their place in Scotland. He was an artist and writer, with a very sensitive and intelligent face, someone to whom I took an immediate liking. He told me his cancer had started in the prostate. He had had that operation, then another when the cancer had spread to the intestine, then he'd had a brain tumor removed. He had been feeling completely normal until a few weeks before when he'd been suddenly stricken with severe headaches and nausea. He'd recently had a CAT scan and been told there was nothing wrong, but he wanted me to tell him what I thought.

When I put my hand on his head, it began vibrating on the side opposite from where he'd had the tumor removed. I felt sure there was a growth, but I didn't like to go against the doctors and alarm him. "There is probably some brain damage after surgery," I told him. From his face, I was sure he knew I suspected cancer.

The very next day his condition deteriorated and he had trouble walking. "You must send for your wife immediately and be readmitted to hospital," I said. At the hospital, he told the doctors I had diagnosed a tumor. When they confirmed my diagnosis with a second scan, he persuaded the doctors to allow me to come to the hospital to treat him. In my experience, this was a very unusual and enlightened attitude for doctors to take.

I went to the hospital twice a day, pouring out all my energy to try to save this man. In the evenings, I treated the other patients Dr. Mookerjee had arranged for me to see, but most of my thoughts were focused on Rory. When he had no more nausea or vomiting and his headaches had stopped, I told him I must return home — I had already stayed several days longer than I'd planned. Rory and his wife both wanted me to stay, but I explained I had to get back to my husband and my patients in India. "We will meet again soon," I encouraged Rory, but he only looked very sad and stared at me as if he would imprint my face on his memory. I felt then he was planning something and that I would never see him again.

When I arrived home I received a wonderful letter from him that I will quote in part:

My Dear Sree:

How can I possibly thank you adequately for your marvellous treatment, and the great privilege you have given me of your friendship in visiting me. In short, I cannot. Yours was a great gift to me and I can only humbly accept it in the same spirit of simplicity in which you gave it.

In his letter, Rory also said he was suffering from a depression he was finding very difficult to overcome, even though the doctors had told him he was cured. "I feel I don't want to go on," he wrote. Within a few

weeks, I heard from Dr. Mookerjee that he was dead, and I was sure
it had not been a normal death. Then I got a letter from his wife. I can
still hardly believe what a terrible end he chose. She told me he
had been very sad and morose when he'd returned from hospital. Early
one morning he had taken his daughter's car, driven to the nearest
underground station and thrown himself under a train. He had left a note
behind, saying he thought this would be the best way to die, quickly, not
lingering on alone. I often look at his picture, and read the book he gave
me, and think about him. So many deaths I have lived through, but his
was one that touched me very deeply.

21

MORE INTERNATIONAL CONFERENCES

In 1983 Dr. Dieter Scheid invited me to give a workshop at the Second Conference on Shamanism and Healing during the first week in June. As before, the meeting was held in Alpbach, Austria, but except for myself, Michael Harner, and the wonderful Don Jose Matsuwa with his interpreter, Brant Secunda, most of the participants were different.

This time, there was a greater emphasis on the therapeutic role of music in healing. The famous flute player, Paul Horn, was one of several musicians who explored the relationship between music, meditation, and movement. In that beautiful natural setting, surrounded by mountains, meadows, and the open blue sky, one is better able to listen to the music of the drumming heart, the music that is always within and around us. Properly in tune, it can help us replace conflict with healthy living.

This year, Alpbach was much more open to our gathering. Early one morning, Paul Horn played his flute in church. I am always powerfully affected in religious structures when my entire body, not just my hand, vibrates. On this occasion, Paul Horn played so beautifully I felt as if my whole soul had mingled with the music of the universe.

I was particularly interested in meeting Joseph Eagle Elk, a medicine man from the Rosebud Sioux Reservation in the United States. With his wife and two followers, he demonstrated how pipes, plants, and materials sacred to the Sioux are used in prayer and healing. Percy Kuphe, a Zulu witch doctor, gave me a private demonstration of how he helps people who come to him by throwing the bones of his ancestors. He told me the bones enable him to speak to the ancestors, who then help him solve his patients' problems and interpret their dreams.

I was scheduled to give a speech, in addition to demonstrating my healing. I had made no notes or other preparations, confident that Sai Baba would again speak through me. When I came into the hall, I found a large crowd waiting to hear me and, quite spontaneously, I decided to speak about the role of suffering in developing the soul. This speech was not taped, but I felt it was better than the one I'd given the year before. I saw men in the audience wiping away tears and several people told me they had felt I was talking about their own lives. One journalist from Munich told my secretary, "Sree was the only natural speaker. She spoke so simply, but it carried the most valuable message of all — that suffering chisels the soul to perfection and brings us closer to God."

To my surprise, just as I began my speech, I saw a friend from India, a big industrialist, enter the hall. For a moment I was put off, because I know he is not a spiritual person. Then I thought, "I have a speech to make, I must not let this upset me."

When I was back in India, this friend came to see us and told my husband about my workshop. "Sree was by far the best speaker," he said. "I was amazed how well she spoke, not at all self-conscious about all the people around her, and no notes; I was really surprised."

At the end of the conference, I was asked to give two more workshops, one at the Coloman Center, near Munich, and the other in Marienhafe Muhle. I was also able to fit in three days at the Eighth International Transpersonal Conference in Davos, chaired by Dr. Burney. I saw Christina and Dr. Grof again and I was interviewed for Swiss television. This was a very busy and tiring three days. In addition to my workshops, Dr. Burney sent me many patients whom I treated in my hotel room. At the farewell dinner, Dr. Burney asked me to stand up in front of everyone. Then he told them, "I am very proud of Sree. She is my special present to this conference."

Dr. Burney pressed me to come to Kyoto, Japan, for the Ninth International Transpersonal Conference in April, 1985. When the time came, I was too busy with patients in India to go and, a year later, I was very sad to hear Dr. Burney had died in his sleep. I lost a good friend and there have been no more of the international transpersonal conferences held since that year.

22

MORE UNUSUAL CASES AND SOME FINAL THOUGHTS

At the time I am finishing this book, I have been healing for more than thirty years and have treated some thirty thousand patients. In spite of all my experience, I am still surprised by the unusual cases that have come and still come to me. Always, I have treated a fair number of children. I am very fond of children and I never have any problem with them being afraid of me. Perhaps they feel more relaxed in the informal atmosphere of my home than in a doctor's office.

Recently, a young father brought his baby girl to me for treatment. A few months after the child was born, she had started passing blood in her stool. The poor little baby had had endless tests, even blood transfusions, but no one had been able to find the cause of the bleeding or locate the area in which the baby felt pain. As I checked her, my hand vibrated over a particular part of the large intestine. I felt something like a balloon there and the baby suddenly screamed with pain. She came for several treatments and after about the fifth visit, a thin, membranelike substance came out in the bloody stool. I believe what felt like a balloon to my hand must have been some kind of pouch inside her large intestine that filled with blood, burst, and filled up again. As soon as the balloonlike membrane came out of her body in the stool the child became peaceful and normal.

Healing Two Children's Ear Problems

Another child I have been very pleased about is the son of a famous Indian eye surgeon. I've known the child's mother since she was very young and some months ago she telephoned to ask if I could help with their son's partial deafness. Apparently, no one had noticed anything was wrong until the boy was about three years old, when they realized he was having trouble speaking properly, some time after he had run a very high fever. "We have taken him to all the specialists and now the doctors say the nerves of the ear are partially dead and there is no possibility of a cure," the mother told me.

"With your husband such a famous surgeon, I know you will have seen all the top doctors," I said, "what do you think I can do for the boy?" She begged me please to just see him and tell her if I agreed it was hopeless.

When she brought her son, Chaitanya, I could hardly understand what he was saying. In particular, he had trouble with the letter "r." I didn't expect to be able to help, but my hand told me the nerves were not dead, it was the phlegm that had hardened. I was not surprised to learn that the child had a long history of bad colds. Even so, I was not at all sure I could help. In spite of all my experience, I am never certain of my healing powers until a cure takes place.

It took three months before his mother and I could be sure he was getting better. What cured him, in addition to my healing, was the application of rock salt formentations (See Chapter 23, " Herbal and Natural Remedies"), which his mother put on his ears each night. The child himself also helped in his own cure.

"Do you think you can help me to make you hear?" I asked Chaitanya.

"Of course," he told me, just like a grown-up. He is an unusually bright and clever child and took great delight in feeling he, too, was helping by each day doing the special yogic finger exercise for deafness, the *shunya mudra* (See Chapter 25).

When his mother finally took him back to the speech therapist, she was astonished. "He doesn't need therapy, he's speaking perfectly," the therapist told her.

One day, his father brought Chaitanya for his treatment. I told him I would have to go on working on the right ear for some time, but I asked if he thought his son's hearing was improved. "It's wonderful, I really can't believe he's so much better," he said.

"This must be a dilemma for you," I teased him, "how can he improve when all the big specialists said he was deaf in that ear for life?"

"I tell you, Mrs. Chakravarti, if I'd heard about this cure happening to anyone but my own son, I would never have believed it," he confessed.

Another similar case came to me very recently. This patient was a three-year-old girl who had lost her voice. She also had suffered from persistent colds, and doctors in India and the United States were recommending surgery for a probable growth in the larynx.

When I examined the child I found her chronic colds and all the antibiotics she'd been given had hardened the phlegm. In only a few treatments I was happy to have her talking and singing, completely cured.

Healing a Perforated Ear Drum

I remember another ear case that was rather unusual. An army officer came to me through his wife, a very good friend. His jeep had been blown up by a mine on the battlefield, and when he was thrown out his ear drum had been perforated. Several surgeons had said the ear was too damaged to be operated on as there was no blood circulating to the area.

I started to give treatments as a favor to my friend and after a few sittings he complained of pain. His wife rang me up in great alarm. "My husband thinks you must have put your finger inside his ear and made it worse. You have such tiny hands, like a child's, do you think it's possible?"

I was very indignant. "Of course I did no such thing," I told her. "He'd better go to an ear, nose, and throat specialist and put his mind at rest."

When the officer saw the ear, nose, and throat surgeon, the surgeon was delighted. "The reason you've got pain there," he explained, "is because the circulation has started again. It's a very good sign. If it continues to heal like this, we'll be able to operate."

When the officer came back to me, I said I wouldn't treat him. "Imagine telling everyone I put my finger in your ear and made the perforation worse," I scolded him. However, I relented and continued the healing until he was able to have the operation successfully.

Treating a Fractured Skull

One of my strangest cases is one that has gone down in medical history. I was asked to treat a plastic surgeon whose skull was fractured when the two-wheeler in which he was traveling was in an accident. He was taken to the hospital in a coma during which the doctors removed several small pieces of bone from his skull. When he regained consciousness, he had no memory of the accident, but he was left with dreadful headaches. After only a few sittings with me, his headaches ceased. However, the doctors still wanted to operate to repair the dura, the tough outer membrane that encases the brain. The operation was to be done by another famous plastic surgeon in an army hospital.

When he opened up the skull the surgeon found that the soft part of the brain where he planned to do the skin graft had repaired itself, a first in medical history. None of the doctors had any theory to account for how this had happened. My patient did not tell them he had had some fifteen sittings with me. Perhaps he was ashamed to mention he had gone to a spiritual healer.

Treating with Sai Baba's Ashes

I treated two strange cases involving mental disturbances, quite unlike any other healing I have done. I always refuse patients with any kind of mental problem, but I was persuaded to see both these cases because I knew the families well. In both instances, I used Sai Baba's ashes in the healing.

The saint's ashes, known as the sacred *vibhuti* of Sai Baba, are known to have some kind of miraculous power. When Sai Baba lived alone in his crumbling mosque in Shirdi, he always kept a fire burning in one corner by feeding it with small pieces of wood. The same fire has been kept alight since his death by visitors to Shirdi who throw their own small pieces of wood on the fire when they come to worship there. The ashes from this fire are in great demand for healing and I usually try to keep a small supply in my home.

The child I treated with the ashes was a little girl who had had a tragic experience. Her step-brother had died in an accident on the playing field, and for some reason they had carried the dead boy's body into the school where she was studying. When the child saw the beloved brother's dead body she fainted, and from that time on she had alternated between being very quiet and having episodes of frighteningly violent behavior. When her family could get no help from doctors, they went to a priest. "She is being haunted by the ghost of her dead brother, and he wants her to join him," he warned them.

I told them straight out I never took such cases, but the family begged me to help — "perhaps the touch of your hand will calm her." I was very nervous about the case and I consulted a friend who is a famous authority on tantric literature. "The child will get cured through the touch of your hand and the presence of Sai Baba," he told me. "Just put her on your bed where you do the healing and pray to Baba."

When the mother brought in the child she looked most abnormal, and I was astonished to see her look at me with such hatred, not like a child's hatred, but like a grown-up's. She absolutely refused to lie down or allow me to put any of the sacred ash from Baba's fire on her forehead, pushing me away with great violence. I told the mother to take her home and let her sleep with the ashes under her pillow for several nights and then bring her back. The next time the child came she was calmer and agreed to lie on the bed. But while I was questioning the mother how long she had been like this, the child suddenly grabbed an ebony elephant and tried to hurl it at the picture of Sai Baba. When the mother took the ornament from her hand, she continued to stare at Baba's picture with great hatred.

We continued with the ashes under her pillow at night and with my hand's vibrations on her head the days she came for treatment. Her violent episodes stopped and she began to play again for the first time. By the time I was able to tell the mother that she need not bring the child anymore, the little girl clung to me and said she never wanted to leave. So ended a most peculiar case.

Another case I treated with the ashes was a young man who worked at a bank and who was in danger of losing his job. "I feel as if two people are struggling together inside my brain, one good and one bad," he told me. "It is so hard to understand, but when I am adding up figures I know which figure is right, but the bad person inside will make me put down the wrong number."

I asked his mother if he had always been like this. She told me he had been a perfectly normal child until he was about eight years old, when he'd been playing with his father's loaded gun. When the gun went off by accident, his father had been killed. The boy had never been able to get over the guilt and his behavior had gradually become more and more strange.

I could only suggest she take some of Sai Baba's ashes home and help sooth her son's troubled sleep by putting ash on his forehead every night at bedtime. After a few months I got a letter from his mother saying he was better and could she have some more of the ashes. Within a year, she wrote to say her son had made a total recovery.

Bringing Peace from Pain

I always find it drains too much of my energy to treat patients in the hospital, but recently I could not refuse a dear friend's request to visit her sister, dying of a brain tumor in a hospital some distance from Delhi. My husband was very upset about my going, he was afraid I would get too tired, but I could not say no.

When I came into the hospital room my friends' sister was semiconscious, but moaning, and one could see from her face that she was in agony. "The doctors say there is nothing they can do to stop the pain," her sisters told me. Immediately I went to their sister's bedside and laid my hand on her head. After about half an hour she stopped crying out and started to breathe peacefully. I came back in the evening and this time when I put my hand on her head, slowly she reached up to take my hand and very slowly she moved it to the other side of her head. After a few minutes, she smiled just the tiniest bit. Next day, she was not groaning at all. I stayed three days, until she was resting peacefully. She died three days later, very tranquil.

I was not able to cure her, but it gave my friends great comfort to know their sister had not died in pain.

A "Miracle" Case

Recently I treated a young boy and I really feel that I can call this patient a "miracle" case. A boy of eleven years old was brought to me from the hospital. He'd had a stroke several days before, but in the hospital the doctors had not been able to do more than recommend physiotherapy and aspirin. Neither had helped, and when the parents brought him to see me, his father had to carry the boy up the stairs.

"Nikhil was hale and hearty in the evening before he had the stroke," they told me. "He played cricket with his friends, but next morning he just could not get up. He could speak, there was nothing wrong with his speech, but he couldn't move his left leg or his left arm."

When I examined him, my hand went to a spot on the brain. "Do you feel the vibration?" I asked the boy. When he said he did, I worked on him for one hour, then I told him to try to sit up on his own. He was not only able to sit up without help, but he could move his left leg and left arm a little.

After the second treatment he was able to stand without support. With the third treatment, he could walk a few steps. By the fourth treatment he was able to run, and my hand stopped vibrating.

A few weeks later they all came to thank me. Nikhil, in particular, wanted to see me again. I consider it truly a miracle cure that Nikhil got well again in only four sittings.

Some Final Thoughts

While I have been writing this book, I have been thinking about so many things. Still I sometimes wonder why I had to suffer the death of our son. Then I remember that pain is the hammer of God which chisels us into greatness. Without suffering we cannot bring out the best part of ourselves. It is like the lamp that gives light, or the incense that gives fragrance only when it burns. Gold can be used only when it has been purified. So it is with our life. Without suffering one cannot reach God. When we suffer, then we try to find Him. We realize He is the only true and permanent thing in this life. He is reality. All the other things are useless and give us only temporary comfort or pleasure. Still we run after the unreal, thinking it to be real.

When I think of suffering, I also remember that part of the inspiration for this book was one of my first patients, a woman who was dying of cancer. Her father asked me to help, he was giving so much money to charity hoping to save her. She was a lovely person, I wanted to give her comfort. Her husband told me bluntly one day, "The doctors have given up hope, you are just wasting your time and energy."

"My job is different from what you imagine," I told him. "I am trying my best to let the candle burn as long as possible." My patient had no idea she was so ill and she seemed to get better each time she saw me.

"The whole day I wait for you," she said. "I anxiously wait to hear your footsteps. The day you don't come I am miserable."

One day I was treating her when some visitors came. I didn't like working in front of them as they didn't understand what I was doing. I was shocked to hear them tell her about "a case like yours of cancer in the uterus, spine, and liver," and how the lady had just died. I could see my patient was stunned — she had had no idea of her disease. She asked her husband to come and carry her from room to room in the house so she could see it for the last time. She wanted me to come with her, but I could not go the whole way, my heart was breaking. The next time I came, the doctors had given her some medicines and she did not even recognize me. Soon after that, she died.

Sometimes I feel cancer is caused by disharmony. This woman had every kind of luxury in her life, but she got no companionship from her husband, his only interest was in making money. Both her children were in boarding school. There was a void in her life. I thought then, in my mind, if I don't write about her, she will get lost. If anyone reads these lines, for a short time she will be living again.

I cannot end my book without saying how important my late husband's support was to my work. In the beginnning, he did not believe in my healing powers and he did all he could to discourage me. This made me sad because all the praise others gave me meant nothing if I did not have his praise. Yet all my life there has been something obstinate in my nature that the more I am opposed, the harder I struggle. Now when I look back, I believe it was God's hand that made my husband oppose my work. If he had praised and encouraged me too much from the first, I might have destroyed my gift with false vanity.

Thinking back, I realize that his later encouragement was the most important thing in my life. He understood and explained to people how my healing energy works better than I can understand and explain it myself. His presence was a blessing that allowed me to work in peace and harmony. I shall never stop missing him.

I began this book with a quotation from my favourite poet, Rabindranath Tagore. I should like to end it with a few lines from his *Gitanjali*:

> *I thought that my voyage had come to its end at the last limit of my power, that the path before me was closed, that provisions were exhausted and the time come to take shelter in a silent obscurity.*

> *But I find that Thy will knows no end in me. When old words die out on the tongue, new melodies break forth from the heart; and where the old tracks are lost, new country is revealed in its wonders.*

Sree in her garden in New Delhi, 1992.

photographer: Olaf Hauge

PART TWO

A Practical Legacy

Self-Healing Techniques
and Remedies

23
HERBAL AND NATURAL REMEDIES

Chapter Summary

1. Amlaki

For weakness of the heart, brain, eyesight, intelligence, and memory; asthma and chronic colds; diabetes

2. Bael Leaves

For diabetes; peptic and gastric ulcers

3. Bindi (okra) and Jamun

To reduce high blood sugar content and control incipient diabetes

4. Bark of Arjun

For heart problems

5. Fenugreek

For anemia; aches and pains; diabetes; intestinal ulcers; fever; high blood pressure; indigestion; loose bowel movements; cosmetic uses

6. Garlic and Onions

Garlic for asthma, emphysema; arteriosclerosis; memory loss; fluid in the joints; lip cancer

Onions for dry cough and hoarse voice; bladder weakness; insomnia; arthritis

7. Kanta Gokhur

For urinary tract and kidney infections

8. Kule Khara

For anemia; as substitute for blood transfusion; herpes ulcers

9. Kulthi

For high blood pressure; reducing cholesterol; kidney ailments and infections; kidney stones

10. Parsley

For kidney cleanser and tonic for thyroid and adrenal glands

11. Soya Beans and Bengal Gram

For lowering cholesterol

12. Spices Used in Healing

Cardamom; cloves; cinnamon; cummin seeds and aniseed; ginger; nutmeg; tumeric

13. Rock Salt

For use as a compress

14. Tulsi

To improve the blood circulation; alleviate cold symptoms; alleviate urinary obstructions due to an infection; help ulcerative colitis

15. Vegetables and Vegetable Juices
Cabbage; carrots; spinach

16. Miscellaneous Additional Remedies

17. Ayurvedic Medicines
Description; uses; where to purchase

Even before I began healing more than thirty years ago, I was always interested in herbal and natural remedies. In India, the ancient traditional Hindu system of medicine is called *ayurveda* — which means life, or vital power, plus knowledge. It is based largely on homeopathy and naturopathy. Over the years I have worked with many traditional doctors who have shared their knowledge with me. I have a library of old ayurvedic texts and I also consult, in particular, the work of a contemporary *ayurvedacharya* (master doctor) based in Calcutta, Shibkali Bhattacharya. His book, *Chiranjeer Bonausdhi*, is a treasury of information on the use of bush and jungle plants in natural cures. Unfortunately, his work has not been translated from Bengali into Hindi or English.

I shall also be forever grateful to a nun I knew in Calcutta, Mother Emmi, who died some years ago. She was a great believer in homeopathic medicines and in a special black plaster developed for a variety of external applications more than fifty years ago in South India by a Roman Catholic priest, Father Causaunal. I heat this plaster and use it as a compress to draw out poisons from the body, particularly for cases of slipped discs, tumors, and abcesses. The plaster works to soften the abcess and draw out the pus without lancing. The plaster is also recommended for skin ulcers, wounds, sores, rheumatic aches and pains, etc., but I have used it mainly to treat the problems I've mentioned above. At the end of this chapter, I give an address where you can order the plaster, and also addresses where you can purchase the various Indian herbal and ayurvedic remedies I recommend.

There are literally hundreds of herbal remedies available in India, but I recommend only those I have used successfully. Following are the herbal cures I particularly recommend, what they should be used for, and how they are prepared.

1. AMLAKI

(Also known as *amla, aunla*).

Botanical Name: *Emblica officinalis.*

This fruit, which resembles a large gooseberry, can be eaten dried or fresh and green in season. Either way, it is full of iron and vitamin C and has a very sour taste.

What Amlaki is good for:

As a general tonic to improve weakness of the heart, brain, eyesight, intelligence, and memory. *Amlaki* is also useful for treating asthma caused by phlegm in the chest; diabetes, and chronic colds.

How to take Amlaki:

Either eat the green fruit daily in season, or drink 1/2 cup of the water in which 8-10 pieces of dried *amlaki* have been soaked overnight.

2. BAEL LEAVES

(The bael tree is also called stone apple tree; *bala* or *bael* in Bengali; *baela* in Marathi; *bilva* in Sanskrit; *bila* in Sindhi; *vilvapazham* in Tamil; *maredu* in Telegu.)

Botanical Name: *Aegle marmelos, corr.*

The bael tree is grown throughout India and the fruit is rich in vitamin C, with a little vitamin B complex. The tree is sacred to Hindus and its leaves are a favorite offering to Lord Shiva, without which his worship is considered incomplete.

Here I write about the use of bael *leaves* only.

What bael leaves are good for:

To cure diabetes and gastric and peptic ulcers.

How to use bael leaves:

(1) **To treat diabetes:** Bael leaves stimulate the pancreas to produce insulin, but should be taken in conjunction with the strict dietary restrictions recommended by the doctor and any allopathic medicines being prescribed.

- **If the patient is NOT taking insulin:** Take 21 fresh young bael leaves, crush them, add the powder from 7 black peppercorns, strain the juice. Take 1 teaspoon of this juice first thing in the morning. If there is more than one teaspoon of juice, wait 10 minutes, then take the rest. For a patient who is not on insulin, one teaspoon daily is enough.

- **If the patient IS taking insulin:** He should take 2-3 teaspoons 2-3 times a day, at any time during the day. As mentioned above, the juice stimulates the production of insulin.

At the end of 15 days, have the blood sugar checked. Always there is an improvement. Take no juice for 15 days, then repeat as necessary. As the condition improves, the dose should be gradually decreased.

(2) To Treat Peptic and Gastric Ulcers: The juice of the bael leaves is very good for treating peptic or gastric ulcers. Soak 7-8 bael leaves overnight in a glass of water. Strain the water and take first thing in the morning on an empty stomach.

Follow this regimen for one month. The bael leaf water forms a coating on the stomach lining that helps heal the ulcer.

3. BARK of ARJUN

(The *arjun* tree or white murdah, is known as *arjun* in Bengali and Marathi; *arjan* in Pushtu; *arjunsadada* in Gujrati; *arjuna* in Sanskrit; *kahu* in Hindustani; *toramatti* in Karnataki; *vellamarda* in Tamil and *maddi* in Telegu.)

Botanical Name: *Terminilia arjuna W & A.*

Arjun trees, which grow throughout most of the Indian subcontinent, can grow as high as 100 feet with a girth of 20 feet. The bark, which is used in Indian herbal medicines, is greyish white, smooth, and about 1/2 inch thick.

What Bark of Arjun is good for:

The bark of the tree is useful as a tonic to treat problems of the heart, such as weakness, palpitations, pains in the heart (angina), etc.

How to prepare Bark of Arjun:

Powder the bark after drying it in the sun.

Boil one tablespoon of powdered bark in 1 cup of milk mixed with 1 cup of water until the mixture is reduced by half. Add honey to sweeten and drink at any time.

Or one may also take the powdered bark by mixing 2 teaspoons of powder in 1 cup of hot milk sweetened with honey to taste. This mixture should be taken first thing in the morning on an empty stomach.

4. BINDI and JAMUN

(The small green pods of the vegetable *bindi* are known as *okra* in English. Jamun fruit is also called *jumbal* fruit, rose apple, or java plum. The tree is native to India and is now found in all tropical regions.)

Botanical Name: Bindi: *Hibiscus esculentus.*
Jamum: *Syzygium cumini* or *Eugenia jambolana.*

What bindi and jamun are good for:

In traditional, or ayurvedic, medicine, both *bindi* and *jamun* are used to reduce sugar in the blood for patients with threatened or actual diabetes.

How to prepare the bindi and jamun mixture:

Select fresh young tender pods of *bindi* (okra). Cut in half lengthwise and boil in 1 cup of water until pods are soft and water reduced to 1/2 cup.

Mix into the well-softened *bindi* and 1/2 cup of water, a 1/2 teaspoon (one gram) of dried, powdered *jamun* fruit. Eat the mixture at one time, anytime during the day.

Have the blood sugar checked before starting this treatment. Continue treatment for 10 days, at which time the blood sugar content will be significantly reduced, assuming of course the patient is following the sensible sugar-free diet normally recommended for diabetics.

Treatment may be discontinued at any time blood sugar is reduced to a safe level and resumed at any time.

5. FENUGREEK

(Also called *methi* in Bengali, Gujarati, Hindustani, and Marathi; *menthya* in Karnataki; *methun* in Punjabi; *medhika* in Sanskrit; *mathi* in Sindhi; *ventayam* in Tamil; *mentula* in Telegu.)

Botanical Name: *Trigonella foenumgraeceum, linn.*

Fenugreek is a very versatile plant. Both its seeds and leaves are used in a wide variety of herbal cures popular in India, Arab countries, and Israel. The leaves of Fenugreek are well known as a winter vegetable and for their curative properties. After flowering, the plant bears seed pods nearly two inches long. When the pods dry, the yellow seeds inside are also used in many remedies.

Fenugreek is prepared in a variety of ways, depending on the ailment to be treated. The leaves can be boiled, infused, or soaked. The seeds can be used when boiled, infused, soaked, roasted, or powdered.

The various applications of fenugreek and how to prepare them are listed below.

(1) Fenugreek for the Treatment of Anemia: Both the leaves and seeds help in the formation of red blood cells.

Use of Fenugreek *Leaves* for Anemia: Make a soft paste of the leaves by cooking a handful of leaves over medium heat in 1 teaspoon of vegetable oil until wilted — 1 to 2 minutes. Then add 1 cup of water and boil until soft, approximately 15 minutes, and eat while still warm. Patients who can use salt may add salt to taste before eating.

This paste can be taken anytime during the day for 15 days after which the blood count should be taken. Patients may continue the treatment until a satisfactory blood count is reached.

Use of Fenugreek *Seeds* for Anemia: This recipe, which uses the seeds, not the leaves, is especially beneficial for a woman after a miscarriage, spontaneous abortion, or childbirth, and for girls at the onset of puberty. Followed carefully, the red blood cells will be built up again in 7 days.

Soak 1 tablespoon of seeds overnight in enough water to cover. In the morning, boil in a covered pot, in the same water, adding a little more water if necessary, until the seeds are tender — approximately one-half hour over medium heat. Add honey to taste and eat the entire mixture.

Test the blood for the red cell count after 7 days.

(2) Use of Fenugreek for Rheumatic Aches and Pains: Roasted fenugreek seeds are very useful for alleviating any kind of aches and pains, such as rheumatism, arthritis, general body aches, etc.

To prepare, the seeds should be roasted on a dry frying pan over medium heat, stirring frequently, until they are crisp. The seeds should then be powdered on a grinding stone or in a blender. Keep the powder in a tightly sealed glass jar.

Take 1 teaspoonful of Fenugreek powder with meals every day for as long as necessary. If the roasted powdered seeds are too bitter for your taste, mix with curds (yogurt) to take away the bitterness.

(3) Use of Fenugreek for Diabetes: Take 25-100 grams (1-4 teaspoons) daily of the roasted powdered seed (see under "Rheumatic Aches and Pains" above for how to prepare). Mix with a little milk and take before breakfast or 1/2 hour after morning tea. Keep extra powder in a tightly sealed glass jar.

This remedy helps in the formation of insulin and may be taken indefinitely without harm.

(4) Taking Fenugreek for Fever: A tea made by pouring boiling water on powdered fenugreek seeds and letting it steep will help cure a fever by acting as a body cleanser.

(5) Using Fenugreek Seeds with Aniseed and Tumeric for Intestinal Ulcers: To cure any kind of intestinal ulcer, soak 2 teaspoons of fenugreek seeds overnight with 1 teaspoon of aniseed in 1/2 glass of water. Strain and drink *only* the water first thing in the morning on an empty stomach. Prepare fresh each night and take for one month or until all the discomfort of the ulcer goes. Repeat any time pain reappears.

The cure will progress more swiftly if one takes at the same time 1 teaspoon of grated raw tumeric (*haldi*). Raw tumeric, which looks like yellow ginger, is available year-round in Calcutta and in Delhi from October through April. Tumeric is important because it helps cure the liver problems invariably associated with ulcers.

(6) Treating High Blood Pressure with Fenugreek: Soak 4 teaspoons of fenugreek seeds in 1/2 liter of water overnight. Drink the water 2-3 times during the day until finished.

Prepare fresh each night and take for 15 days. Then have your blood pressure checked. This remedy is particularly helpful taken in conjunction with *kulthi* water (see section on *kulthi* below).

(7) Using Fenugreek to Treat Indigestion: Make a paste by cooking a handful of leaves in 1 teaspoon of oil until wilted (1-2 minutes) then adding 1/2 cup of water and boiling about 15 minutes until the leaves are soft. If the patient can tolerate salt, add salt to taste. Take a teaspoonful of the paste after meals whenever necessary

(8) Using Fenugreek to Cure Loose Bowels: Soak 1 teaspoon of Fenugreek seed in a little curd (yogurt). Take first thing in the morning and at bedtime. Repeat for a few days until the problem disappears.

(9) Using Fenugreek for Cosmetic Purposes:

For the complexion: Make a paste of 1 to 2 cups of fresh leaves and a little water by grinding the leaves on a grinding stone or putting leaves and water in a blender. Apply the paste before bedtime for 1/2 hour, then wash off in lukewarm water.

The paste acts as a cleanser and is good for wrinkles, pimples, and blackheads.

For the hair: A paste to keep hair soft and to preserve its natural color may be made from fresh fenugreek leaves or seeds. Prepare a soft paste from the leaves (as above, under "For the Complexion") and apply regularly to the scalp for 1/2 hour before washing.

To make a paste from the seeds, soak 1 tablespoon of seeds overnight in warm water. In the morning, add a little milk and grind together or mix in a blender. Use as above.

6. GARLIC and ONIONS

Garlic

Garlic is a herb that is rich in vitamins A, B, C, and D. It contains phosphorus, calcium, sulphur, and potassium.

The only problem with garlic is the unpleasant smell it can leave on the breath, particularly uncooked garlic. To avoid the smell, soak peeled garlic pods overnight in a little curd (yogurt).

(1) Garlic as a Remedy for Asthma: Boil 2 to 3 pods of peeled garlic in 1/2 cup of vinegar until just tender. Mix with a little honey to sweeten. Chew and swallow. Take daily, at anytime during the day.

Or at bedtime, simmer 2-3 cloves of peeled garlic in 1/2 cup of milk until tender. Chew and swallow.

If taken regularly, this use of garlic will reduce attacks of asthma.

(2) Garlic as a Remedy for Emphysema: Crush a few cloves of peeled garlic in a garlic press. Add 5 to 7 drops of garlic juice to 1/2 cup of cold milk. Drink once every day at anytime during the day. One may get rid of the unpleasant smell, as mentioned above, by soaking the peeled cloves overnight in curd (yogurt).

(3) Garlic as a Remedy for Arteriosclerosis: Garlic is helpful in reducing arteriosclerosis (narrowing of the arteries through build-up of fatty deposits).

Soak 2 pods of peeled garlic overnight in curd (yogurt). Cut into small pieces and swallow without chewing.

(4) Garlic as a Remedy for Memory Loss: To improve memory loss, at bedtime chew and swallow one or two pods of peeled garlic that have been soaked during the day in curd (yogurt) to eliminate the smell. Afterwards, drink a little warm milk.

(5) Garlic as a Remedy for Fluid of the Joints: Prepare a garlic paste by crushing peeled cloves of garlic. Rub the paste on the joints a few times daily to obtain relief.

(6) Garlic as a Remedy for Lip Cancer: Prepare a garlic paste by crushing peeled pods. Apply paste to the cancer and it will heal very fast.

Onions

Like garlic, onion is a herb that may be used in a variety of cures:

(1) Onion as a Remedy for Dry Cough: A dry cough is due to phlegm in the chest. Chop 1 medium size onion into fine pieces. Boil the onion in 1 cup of olive oil until the oil is brown. Strain and keep the oil in a tightly sealed glass jar. Massage the throat, chest, and back with the oil and wipe off after a few minutes with a rag or tissue. Apply as needed until the cough is better.

(2) Onions as a Remedy for Hoarse Voice: Mix 2 teaspoons of onion juice with an equal quantity of pure honey. Warm and drink it.

(3) Onions as a Remedy for Bladder Weakness: For problems of urine retention, take 1 teaspoon of onion juice daily. Taken regularly, onion juice will cure this weakness.

(4) Onions as a Remedy for Insomnia: Mix 2 teaspoons of grated onion with 2 teaspoons of curd (yogurt) and take at bedtime.

(5) Onions and Tumeric Paste for Arthritis: I was once able to completely unlock an old man's arthritic knees with this paste.
Make a paste of 3 parts tumeric (*haldi*), 1 part onion, ground together in a mixer. Apply liberally to the affected joint and wrap tightly in plastic so that the paste does not migrate to your clothes. Leave on all day and wash off carefully before going to bed. Keep applying until the pain is alleviated.

7. KANTA GOKHUR

Botanical Name: *Tribulus terrestris.*

Kanta gokhur is a thorny herb common throughout India. There are two forms of the gokhur herb: the larger variety is called *kabli gokhur* and the smaller, *kanta ghokur*. The dried burr-like seeds of both plants are used in herbal remedies for renal and kidney ailments, but I prefer the remedies that use the smaller variety of *kanta ghokur*. Using the juice prepared from kanta ghokur in conjunction with melon and cucumber juices, the patient with kidney and renal complaints will show dramatic improvement.

(1) *Kanta Gokhur* as a Remedy for SERIOUS Urinary Tract or Kidney Infections: First powder the seeds by grinding, then soak 2 teaspoons of this powder in 2 cups of water overnight. In the morning, reduce the liquid to 1 cup by boiling. Strain and drink 1/2 cup of the warmed liquid first thing in the morning on an empty stomach. Drink the other 1/2 warmed at bedtime. (If it is more convenient to prepare in the evening, soak the powder during the day and prepare as above at night.) In very hot weather, keep the second 1/2 cup in the refrigerator and warm before drinking.

After 10 days, test the urine to see if the kidney infection is cured.

(2) *Kanta Gokhur* for MILD Kidney Infections: Prepare 1/2 portion of the mixture as above. Drink twice a day, morning and evening, for 10 days.

(3) *Kanta Gokhur* for Cloudy Urine in Men: Cloudy urine in men is due to prostate gland trouble. Take 1/2 teaspoon of *kanta gokhur* powder in a little water morning and evening until the urine is clear. It may be taken before or after meals.

8. KULE KHARA

(*Kule khara* is the Bengali name. This herb is also known as *Talmakhna* in Hindi.)

Botanical Name: *Asteracantha longifolia nees.*, family of *Acanthacea.*

This plant grows in the paddy fields of Assam and Bengal during the rainy season in winter. It is a truly remarkable herb, little known outside those two areas. I have always been able to obtain this herb in the Gariahata market near Ballygunge in Calcutta. When available, it is amazingly effective in curing anemia, particularly for patients who cannot tolerate iron. I have given it to so many people, even those with a blood count of 4 (normal is 11-12) with excellent results. It is also useful in building up the blood so that a blood transfusion is not necessary. In many ways, I consider this latter use to be the most important one.

(1) *Kule Khara* as a Remedy for Anemia:
Crush a good handful of leaves to yield 4 teaspoons of juice. Warm a little and drink 2 teaspoons at anytime during the day. Drink the other 2 at bedtime.
After 7 days, the blood count will go up.

(2) *Kule Khara* Substituting for a Blood Transfusion: This herb, which is both safe and economical, can be used instead of a blood transfusion.
Prepare as for anemia above. In 7 days the blood count will go up.

(3) *Kule Khara* and Tumeric as a Remedy for Herpes Ulcers:
Grind together, in equal proportions, the leaves of fresh *kule khara* and raw grated tumeric. Applied to a herpes ulcer, the paste gives immediate relief and leads to a fast healing of the ulcer.

9. KULTHI

(Also known as horse gram in English; *kulthi dal* in Hindi; *kulthi kalai* in Bengali; *mulher* in Malyalam; *kallu* in Tamil; *ulavalu* in Telegu.)

Botanical Name: *Dolichos bifiorus*

Kulthi is widely grown throughout India and drinking the water obtained by soaking *kulthi* grain overnight is one of the remedies I recommend most often, particularly for patients with kidney ailments, high blood pressure, and/or cholesterol problems.

How to Prepare and Use Kulthi:

First clean the grain: Before drinking the water from *kulthi* grain, the grain must be cleaned with a soft dry cloth — not washed — and any impurities removed. The grain must not be washed because water removes the valuable coating of the grain that aids in curing. One pound of grain will last a patient several months.

Store the cleaned grain in a cool place in an air-tight container: I keep mine in a plastic bag inside a metal tin. The grain *must not* be in contact with metal when it is wet or being soaked.

Preparing *Kulthi* water: Soak 1 tablespoon of *kulthi* grain overnight in a glass of water covered with a piece of cheesecloth. In the morning, the water should be drunk after stirring thoroughly with a plastic spoon — not a metal one. The water will have a faint, not unpleasant, taste of grain.

The glass should then be filled again with water two more times and the water drunk at noon and in the evening before discarding the grain and starting the course for the next day. In very hot summer weather, you can drink the water every two hours.

I have found *kulthi* water particularly useful for the following ailments:

(1) *Kulthi* as a Remedy for High Blood Pressure: Regular use of *kulthi* water lowers high blood pressure significantly.

Test your blood pressure before and after one month of use. Blood pressure will invariably be lower, sometimes dramatically so.

(2) *Kulthi* Water to Reduce Cholesterol: Blood circulation improves with the use of *kulthi* water because it "melts" the fat in the system. Test blood cholesterol before and after three months of use.

(3) *Kulthi* Water as a Remedy for Kidney Ailments and Kidney Infections: Regular daily use of *kulthi* water flushes out the kidneys and keeps them healthy.

However, for patients with any kind of kidney problem, I also strongly recommend they drink 6 to 8 glasses of water a day, in addition to the *kulthi* water.

Water flushes out the kidneys and is one of the most effective remedies easily available to all of us.

(4) *Kulthi* Water as a Remedy for Kidney Stones: I strongly recommend drinking *kulthi* water to prevent the formation of kidney stones in patients with a history of kidney-stone formation, or to rid themselves of a formed stone.

I find the cure is hastened if one takes the *kulthi* water in conjunction with Cystone®, a preparation of the Himalaya Drug Company of Bangalore, a long established and highly reputable Indian manufacturer of ayurvedic medicines. The company's address is given at the end of this chapter. Another excellent ayurvedic medicine for general kidney problems is Turaico®. I also list an address where Turaico® can be ordered.

10. PARSLEY

Parlsey is not an indigenous Indian herb, but it is now widely grown in India and its many beneficial uses have long been known in Europe where it originated.

Parsley as a Kidney Cleanser and Tonic for the Thyroid and Adrenal Glands:

I have found that parsley juice is very valuable as a kidney cleanser that keeps the kidneys working well. It also has properties that help the adrenal and thyroid glands to function better.

To prepare, place a handful of parsley in a saucepan and cover with water — none of the parsley leaves should be showing above the water. Boil for just a few minutes. Take off the stove. When cool, strain the juice into a glass container. This juice may be drunk by itself at any time during the day, or in conjunction with other fruit and vegetable juices.

11. SOYA BEANS and BENGAL GRAM

(Soya beans are also know as *bhat*, and Bengal gram as *channa* in Hindi or chick peas in English).

Botanical Name: Soya beans: *Glycine max mere*.
Bengal gram: *Cicer arietinum, linn.*

I sometimes recommend a combination treatment of soya beans and Bengal gram to lower the cholesterol count.

(1) Alternating Beans with Gram to Lower Cholesterol: Select 12-15 soya beans, wash thoroughly and soak overnight. In the morning, again wash them and eat the raw beans at breakfast, chewing very well. *Do not take more than 12-15 beans at one time.*

After 15 days, prepare Bengal gram the same way, using 12-15 pieces of gram each time. Chew well. *Do not take more than 12-15 pieces at one time.*

Test blood cholesterol before starting the course, and at the end of the 30 days of 15 days on soya beans and 15 days on Bengal gram. If the cholesterol count is down, discontinue the treatment.

12. USE of SPICES in HEALING

Cardamom

Use the cardamoms with the thick brown skin, not the smaller, thin-skinned variety.

For a complete bowel movement: Grind 2 large cardamoms in their skins in a little water. Mix with 1 cup of hot water. Strain and drink the warm water. Immediately patients will feel the need to empty their bowels and will have a full movement.

Cloves

Cloves can be used to alleviate toothache. Wash the mouth with warm water, then apply 2-3 crushed cloves to the root of the affected tooth.

Cinnamon

For toothache: Powdered cinnamon will also help toothache applied to the root of the affected tooth after washing out the mouth with warm water.

For piles: Mix 1/4 teaspoon of powdered cinnamon with 1 teaspoon of butter or margarine and take twice daily. One must do this for some time to get a complete cure.

For persistent headache: Use only 1/4 teaspoon of powdered cinammon mixed with 1 tablespoon of butter and apply to the temples and forehead just above the ears. The effect will be very soothing.

Cumin Seeds and Aniseed

Cumin as a general tonic: Soak 2 teaspoons of cumin seed in a glass of water overnight. Strain and drink the water first thing in the morning with a little honey to sweeten.

Cumin or aniseed for digestion: Digestion of food will be helped by chewing very thoroughly 1 teaspoon of aniseed or cumin seed after a meal. The seeds are more pleasant to eat if they have been roasted on a dry pan.

Ginger

Ginger is a versatile spice that has many curative uses.

For nephritis: 1 teaspoon of ginger powder mixed with any food taken once daily helps to cure this kidney ailment.

For colic, diarrhea, dysentery, headache, neuralgia, toothache, and rheumatism: Dilute 1/3 teaspoon of powdered ginger in 1 pint of water. Take a wineglassful three times a day until symptoms depart.

Ginger used as a fomentation: According to the area to be treated, boil a piece of ginger in a bag, wring out the water, and apply the hot bag with the ginger in it to the affected part.

Nutmeg

Nutmeg can be used as a remedy to alleviate the pain from arthritis, spondylitis, etc. Boil 3/4 cup of butter or ghee (clarified butter). Add to the boiled butter a large, finely powdered nutmeg. Store oil in a glass jar when cool. Shake before applying because the powder will sink to the bottom.

13. ROCK SALT

(Sometimes called mountain salt)

I strongly recommend the use of this coarse salt readily available in India and in health food stores abroad, as a mild treatment with definite curative properties.

I use the heated salt in a compress to treat slipped discs, spondylitis (inflammation of the vertebrae), earache or impaired hearing, sinus, or for any type of pain or inflammation, *except* toothache and pains or inflammations of the skull.

For toothache, it is best to use a hot-water gargle. One should never use indirect heat, such as a salt fermentation or Father Causunal's plaster.

To prepare a rock salt compress: Crush about 500 grams of the coarse salt into small pieces, then heat in a frying pan over a high heat until very hot. Empty the hot salt into a very thick bandage — 2 to 3 layers of muslin or some thick cloth. Tie with tape to ensure you maintain the heat for at least one hour. Place a towel on the area to be treated and then apply the rock salt compress. Keep on the affected area until the salt cools.

14. TULSI

(*Tulsi* is the plant's name in Hindustani. It is also known as *Babui-tulsi* in Bengali; *Sabje* in Gujrati; *Ram Kasturi* in Karnataki; *Hazbo* in Kashmiri;

Sabza in Marathi; *Bisva-tulsi* in Sanskrit; *Sabajhi* in Sindhi; *Bhu-tulsi* in Telegu).

Botanical Name: *Ocimum basilicum, linn.*

Tulsi is a plant sacred to Hindus, and the leaves are used in daily worship as an offering to Lord Shiva. Many people grow *tulsi* in their gardens, or in pots inside their homes and it is frequently planted in the grounds of Hindu temples. *Tulsi* leaves and seeds both have a number of important uses in herbal cures.

Tulsi Used to Improve Blood Circulation

Wash and chew 15-20 of the freshly picked leaves for several minutes. Swallow only the juice. This will act as a general tonic, in addition to improving the circulation of the blood.

Tulsi Used to Alleviate Cold Symptoms

For blocked nose: Wrap dried seeds or a mixture of leaves and dried seeds in a piece of muslin cloth and inhale to help unblock the nostrils.

For dry cough: Boil a glassful of water in which there are 5 *tulsi* leaves and 5 black peppercorns until the water is reduced to 1/2 glass. Add a little honey to sweeten and drink as hot as possible. Use until the cough disappears.

Tulsi for Urinary Obstruction Caused by Infection

When there is a problem in passing urine, soak 4 teaspoons of *tulsi* seeds in 2 cups of warm water for 2 hours. Strain the seeds, then crush or mash them, and return to the same water in which they were soaked. Add a little honey and take 4 times a day until urine can be passed easily.

Tulsi for Ulcerative Colitis

Take 21 fresh *tulsi* leaves, grind to a paste, mix with a little curd (yogurt) and take first thing in the morning.

One must follow this regimen for 40 days. It needs patience, but the cure will be permanent.

15. VEGETABLES and VEGETABLE JUICES with HEALING PROPERTIES

Cabbage

Cabbage in its raw state is high in choline, iodine, and sulfur. Cabbage cleanses the intestinal tract, bolsters the immune system, and is helpful in preventing infection. For the best health results, cabbage should be eaten *raw* and *without salt or vinegar*, or taken as *juice* from raw cabbage.

Cabbage juice can also be mixed with spinach and carrot juice. It is also helpful in a diet to cure ulcers when a 1/2 a cup of cabbage juice can be sipped during the day.

If stomach gas results from drinking cabbage juice, this indicates an abnormal bowel condition.

Carrots

The carrot is a powerful cleansing food, rich in alkaline elements that purify and revitalize the blood. It nourishes the entire system and helps to maintain the acid-alkaline balance in the body. Nutritionally, the carrot is rich in vitamin A and carrot juice is an excellent tonic for toning up the whole nervous system. It adds strength to the brain and body. It also improves eyesight.

Mix 1/2 cup of carrot juice in 1 cup of warm milk for an easy tonic that may be drunk at any time.

Spinach

Uncooked, spinach is rich in oxalic acid, a valuable stimulant in the bowel and stomach. *Spinach should never be cooked or heat-processed.* Cooking converts its oxalic acid content into dangerous inorganic crystals that cause kidney pain.

Spinach juice is the ideal cleanser of the intestinal tract. It also regenerates the stomach, duodenum, and small bowel lining. It is also used for loss of vigor, impaired heart function, headaches, and blood pressure changes.

Spinach juice added to raw carrot juice provides one of the most effective and potent health drinks available.

16. MISCELLANEOUS ADDITIONAL REMEDIES

Alum

Alum as a remedy for inflammation of the cervix: Tie a 1/2 teaspoon of alum powder in a soft muslin cloth. Insert into the uterus. Change daily and use for 5-6 days. This will reduce the inflammation that hinders pregnancy.

Glycerine

For gum boils: Use pure glycerine to massage the gums.

Olive Oil and Honey

For gastric and duodenal ulcers: Mix 1/2 teaspoon of pure olive oil and 1/2 teaspoon of honey. Take on an empty stomach first thing in the morning for one month.

Powdered Tablets of Milk of Magnesia

To cure black or brown spots on face or body: Powder 1 tablet of milk of magnesia and mix the powder with a little lime juice. Apply the mixture at bedtime. It may sting a little, but the spot will vanish in a few days.

Tea Leaves and Tea Water

For a quick cure for conjunctivitis (inflammation of the eye): Use an eye bath to bathe the eye 2-3 times in an equal mix of cold tea and pure rose water. Then apply a formentation of weak tea leaves to the closed eye on cottonwool soaked in lukewarm tea. This treatment will cure conjunctivitis in one day.

Addresses Where Herbal and Natural Remedies May Be Purchased

Father Causaunal's (French) Plaster

Causaunal Plaster Makers
Chemmarkudi Road
Tamil Nadu
South India 629001

Ayurvedic Medicines

Today's ayurvedic medicines are based on ancient ayurvedic practice, but nowadays the mixtures of natural ingredients are scientifically formulated to assure uniform and consistent quality. In these combinations of natural herbs, no one ingredient dominates. Instead, they act together to enhance the value of the whole.

- *Abana®* is a cardiac tonic that protects the heart, guards against circulatory problems and wards off the fears and anxieties that often lead to cardiac neurosis.
- *LIV.52®* is primarily a mixture of the extracts of seven indigenous Indian herbs and minerals. It serves to keep the liver functioning at its best; protects the liver from the effects of chemical, heavy metal, and radiation toxicity; helps the liver in time of infections and chemical stress, and serves as an adjunct to various forms of chemotherapy. Since its introduction internationally in 1956, its manufacturers estimate it has been used by more than 60 million people worldwide.
- *Cystone®* keeps the kidneys and the urinary tract flushed and working at optimum efficiency.

Manufacturer of *Abana®*, *LIV.52®*, and *Cystone®*:

The Himalayan Drug Company
Makali, Nelamangala
Bangalore 562 123
India

U.S.A./Canada Importer of *Abana®*, *LIV.52®*, and *Cystone®*:

Ethnobotanica Limited
2897 152nd N.E.
Redmond, Washington 98052
Telephone: 1-800-886-3479
Fax: (206) 869-4231

- *Turaico®* combines five well-known ayurvedic drugs, and is used as a diuretic and as a urinary antiseptic.

Manufacturer of *Turaico®*

J & J De Chane Laboratories Private, Ltd.
4-1-324 Residency Road
Hyderabad 500-001
India

There is no U.S.A./Canada importer of J & J De Chane medicines.

Addresses where one can buy other Indian herbal remedies covered in this chapter:

1. Bark of *Arjun*:

Ram Niwas Jagdish Prasad
40/8 Subhash Market
Kotia Mubarak Pur.
New Delhi 110003
India

2. *Kanta Gokar*, *Kulthi*, Rock Salt, etc.

Goyal Provision Store
H-236-237 Subhash Market, K. M., Pur.
New Delhi 110003
India

24

CORRECT BREATHING AND GOOD HEALTH:

The Prana and Self-Healing

Special Yoga Breathing Exercises

Correct whole-lung breathing, neglected by so many people, is basic to health. Breathing is one of the few wholly automatic bodily functions we can easily learn to control and the benefits of correct breathing — whether one is sick or well — cannot be overestimated. Truly it is said in yoga, "breath is life."

There are many different breathing exercises one can do, but I shall only recommend here the four I have personally found most beneficial in healing.

- *Rhythmic or equalizing breathing* should be practised daily to cleanse the lungs, and should always be done before a special breathing exercise.
- *Nostril Breathing* should be done daily to purify the nerves.
- *Psychic or revitalizing breathing* is recommended for all patients with life-threatening illnesses.
- *Funnel tongue breathing* is only for those suffering from an *under*-active thyroid.

Rhythmic or equalizing breathing

Sit or stand comfortably, with the spine straight, facing the early morning sun if possible.

Inhale through the nose to count of 7. Hold your breath for the count of 1. Exhale through your nose to the count of 7. Wait for the count of 1, then repeat the whole rhythm. Establishing this rhythm — 7:1:7:1 is the rhythm I personally use — is called equalizing the breath. When you breath IN, it is important to fill your whole lungs. To make sure you are doing this correctly, place your hand lightly on your abdomen to check that it distends as you are breathing IN.

When you breath OUT, gently draw in your stomach towards your spine. This forces the air into your upper lungs as you exhale.

I've gone into such detail as I am always surprised at how many people who haven't studied yoga have no idea how to breathe correctly. When you practice this rhythmic breathing daily, preferably in the early morning, you will soon find that this method of inhaling and exhaling becomes completely automatic.

Rhythmic breathing helps draw you into meditation and should *always* be done three to four times before you begin the special breathing exercises described below.

Nostril Breathing

In yoga, the left nostril represents the moon (coolness); the right nostril represents the sun (heat).

Although our breathing may vary during the day, it is always correct to breathe through the left nostril (the moon) during the day and the right nostril (the sun) by night. The moon breath is also always prominent when we do any creative work — painting, singing, etc. When we are angry or excited, we breathe through the right nostril; when we are in harmony with ourselves, we breathe through the left nostril. One can always change the nostril breath by closing one nostril and switching the breath to the other.

Yoga recommends alternate nostril breathing to purify the nerves. This is how this exercise should be done — much harder to describe than to do:

With closed mouth, take two or three "rhythmic breaths" (see preceding section).

Now place your thumb and forefinger above your nose. First stop the right nostril by blocking it with your thumb and inhale deeply through the left nostril. Immediately switch to blocking your left nostril with your forefinger and expel your breath through your right nostril.

Now breathe in deeply through the right nostril while the left nostril remains blocked. Immediately switch to blocking the right nostril while expelling air through your left nostril.

Repeat this alternate nostril breathing five times several times a day, starting in the morning.

Psychic or Revitalizing Breathing

I strongly recommend psychic breathing to all my patients with life-threatening illnesses. By itself, this exercise will not cure the illness, but it will help speed recovery.

First cleanse your lungs by breathing rhythmically three to four times, then inhale deeply and hold your breath as long as you can. Now brace your tongue against your palate, open your mouth and exhale as forcefully as you can, making a loud noise that sounds like steam escaping from a steam engine. Practice this exercise 50-100-200 times daily with patience and faith. You will be amazed at how much energy will be generated for you.

Also vitally important for patients with life-threatening illnesses is the practice of a simple yogic finger posture, the *prana mudra*, described in Chapter 26.

Funnel Breathing for Patients With an Under-active Thyroid

This breathing exercise should *only* be practiced by patients with an *under*-active thyroid.

First cleanse the lungs with three to four rhythmic breaths in the 7:1:7:1 rhythm I recommend.

Now fold your tongue so that it forms a funnel and let it protrude slightly from between your lips. Use your folded tongue to draw air into your lungs with a hissing sound. Hold your breath as long as you can without discomfort, then exhale gently through both nostrils.

Repeat the cycle 10 times, morning and evening, for 2 weeks. Remember, always purify the lungs with 3-4 equalizing breaths before beginning the breathing exercise cycle.

To help correct for under-activity of the thyroid, you should also practice the *prana-mudra*, see Chapter 26, at least once daily.

At the end of two weeks of doing these exercises, go to your doctor to have him check your condition. If he says you are better, you may discontinue the cycle and resume it whenever needed.

The Prana and Self-Healing

In this book I frequently refer to the *Prana* or life force. *Prana* is a central concept in Hindu philosophy that underlies the practice of yoga. I thought that learning a little about this philosophy would help the reader understand my own ideas on healing, and why correct breathing, exercise and meditation are so important in self-healing because they provide a vital link to the *Prana*.

In his famous work of Hindu philosophy, *Raja Yoga or Conquering the Internal Nature*,* the great Indian saint Swami Vivekananda describes how the whole universe is composed of two substances: *Akasha*, the inert material from which everything in the universe is created, and *Prana*, the vital life force that activates the universe. To quote directly from his book in the chapter entitled "Prana".

It is the Akasha that becomes the air, that becomes the liquids, that becomes the solids; it is the Akasha that becomes the sun, the earth, the moon, the stars, the comets; it is the Akasha that becomes the human body, the animal body, the plants, every form that we see, everything that can be sensed, everything that exists. It cannot be perceived; it is so subtle that it is beyond all ordinary perception; it can only be seen when it has become gross, has taken form. At the

* *Raja Yoga or Conquering the Internal Nature* by Swami Vivekanada is published by Avaita Ashram, Publications Department, 5 Entally Road, Calcutta 700 014, India.

beginning of creation there is only this Akasha. *At the end of the cycle the solids, the liquids, and the gases all melt into the* Akasha *again, and the next creation similarly proceeds out of this* Akasha.

By what power is this Akasha *manufactured into this universe? By the power of* Prana. *Just as* Akasha *is the infinite, omnipresent material of this universe, so is this* Prana *the infinite, omnipresent manifesting power of this universe . . . . Out of this* Prana *is evolved everything that we call energy, everything that we call force. It is the* Prana *that is manifesting as motion; it is the* Prana *that is manifesting as gravitation, as magnetism. It is the* Prana *that is manifesting as the actions of the body, as the nerve currents, as thought force. From thought down to the lowest force, everything is but the manifestation of* Prana.

In Hindu philosophy, disease comes about when there is any impediment to the *Prana* flowing through the body — whether the impediment is physical or mental. Body and mind interact and neither can be healthy unless both are healthy.

To keep one's mind and body healthy, one should do one's best to attain knowledge and control of the *Prana*: For the body, through correct breathing and yoga exercises, and for the mind, through meditation.

As Vivekananda says, "The most obvious manifestation of the *Prana* in the human body is in the motion of the lungs. If that stops, as a rule all the other manifestations of force in the body will stop." The aim of controlling our breathing, then, is to bring us into harmony with ourselves and the whole universe. In the same way, yoga exercises (*asanas*) are designed to control the body so that all the atoms of the body are open to nourishment through the *Prana*.

Meditation could be described as the search for truth, the mental discipline that allows our mind to experience the *Prana*. The word "yoga" means union with oneself. When we meditate, we start the inner journey of our mind to control our thoughts, scattered in all directions in our complex modern society. Only by the practice of meditation does the ripening of the soul take place. We may call this self-realization, we may call this union the quest for truth. The experience of seeing the inner light, granted to only the few through God's grace, is like seeing one hundred suns. To quote again from the *Raja Yoga*:

> *The little wave of Prana that represents our own energies, mental and physical, is the nearest to us of all the waves in the infinite ocean of Prana. If we can succeed in controlling that little wave, then alone can we hope to control the whole Prana.*

In terms of physical health, mastering the *Prana* by mind and body exercises is the best way to stay healthy and to help in self-healing. As a holistic healer, my work is to arouse and rechannel the *Prana* in patients who come to me for help.

In metaphysical terms, mastering the *Prana* represents bringing oneself into harmony with the whole universe and by so doing to develop the soul. In Vivekananda's words:*

> *Each soul is potentially divine.*
>
> *The goal is to manifest this divinity within by controlling nature, external and internal.*
>
> *Do this either by work, or worship, or psychic control, or philosophy — by one, or more, or all of these — and be free.*
>
> *This is the whole of religion. Doctrines, or dogmas, or rituals, or books, or temples, or forms, are but secondary details.*

---

* (From Swami Vivekananda's Commentaries on *Yoga-Sutras*, 11.25)

25
ASANAS:
Healing Exercises for the Body

Of the many hundreds of yoga exercises (*asanas*), I recommend only those that I know from my own experience in healing to have a preventative or curative effect.

It is always better to study yoga with an instructor to be sure you are exercising correctly, but three of the exercises I suggest can be done quite safely on your own. I would *not* recommend you practise the shoulder stand (*sarvangasana*) without expert help. Until you have fully mastered the procedure, you could have a damaging fall.

The *asanas* I recommend are the following:

- *Sarvang asana*: For under-activity of the thyroid. The shoulder stand, by putting pressure on the thyroid, helps to activate it.
- *Paschimottan asana*: For diabetes. This exercise helps activate the pancreas that produces insulin.
- *Shashank asana*: For asthma. With experience, the onset of an attack can be controlled by practising this *asana*.
- *Siddh asana*: For high blood pressure. The "coronary posture" is effective for patients with high blood pressure.
- *Sarpa asana*: For spinal problems.
- *An asana I invented for slipped discs*.

1. Sarvang Asana

(For under-activity of the thyroid)

Note: You should not practise this exercise without expert guidance and assistance.

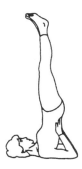

Lie flat on the floor with your head in line with your body. Cleanse the lungs with rhythmic breathing, then inhale deeply. While exhaling slowly, raise the legs, hips, and trunk in a continuous motion until vertical, with your chin pressed firmly into your chest. Make sure your body is in a straight line. You should be resting on the back of the head, the neck, the shoulders, and the upper arms.

In the beginning, you will probably need to support your back with your hands. As you get better, you will be able to stretch out your arms on the floor. Come down very carefully, curling up the legs and returning gradually to the floor. Keep your neck on the floor as you return to the starting position.

When you first start, you will probably only be able to hold this pose for about 10 seconds. As you get better, you will find you can easily hold it for three minutes or more.

2. Paschimottan Asana

(for diabetes)

Sit on the floor with your legs straight in front of you. Practise rhythmic breathing, then inhale slowly, raising your arms straight above your head. Stretch up to straighten your spine as much as you can. Now exhale slowly and bend forward from the hips, keeping your back straight, until your head touches your shins and you can grasp your toes with your hands. Pull your toes as if you were trying to put your head on them.

Stay in this position for a few seconds when you first start, breathing normally. Come up slowly, keeping your hands above your head. When you reach the sitting position, straighten your spine. Now slowly lower your arms to your sides.

You may find this exercise very diffcult when you start and you will probably not be able to reach your toes with your hands. Just stretch as far as you can, concentrating on keeping your back straight. As you practise, your body will become more flexible and you will be able to do it better and better. As noted, the *Paschimottan Asana* activates the pancreas to produce insulin.

3. Shashank Asana

(For asthma)

If you suffer from asthma, you can produce adrenelin — the cure your doctor uses for serious attacks — by practising this posture.

Sit on your feet, raise your hands over your head, then bend forward so that your forehead is on the floor with your arms stretched out in front of you. This pose will activate the adrenal glands to produce adrenalin.

Relax and hold this posture for 10 to 15 minutes. When you know an attack is coming on by the heaviness in your chest and the shortening of your breath, use this posture to control the attack.

4. Siddh Asana

(For high blood pressure)

Siddh asana is the posture in which we sit for meditation. In this posture, you sit upright with the spine very straight. The left foot is placed beneath the perineum, with the right foot over the left. Your legs should be as flat on the floor as possible. The hands may lie flat on the knees, or you may practice one of the *mudras* (healing finger postures) I describe in Chapter 26.

There are many advantages to this posture, such as curing stiffness in the knees, but I particularly recommend it to help bring down high blood pressure.

5. Sarpa Asana

(For spinal problem, slipped discs, spondylitis)

I have found the *Sarpa Asana* (serpent posture) to be very helpful in treating patients with slipped discs and spondylitis (inflammation of the spine).

Lie flat on your stomach on the floor, legs together, with your forehead touching the floor. Your pelvis and knees should be flat on the floor, but your feet should be arched upward with just your toes touching the ground. Your arms should be bent so that your hands rest on the floor, parallel with your body, at shoulder height. Breathe normally.

Take a slow deep breath and gradually push yourself up on your arms to raise your head and shoulders a few inches off the floor, arching your head and spine as far backwards as possible while keeping your abdomen firmly on the ground. This arching loosens stiffened back muscles and exercises the cranial muscles.

Keeping the same position, let your breath out and then again inhale deeply. Hold this breath while very slowly turning your head as far as possible to the left, so that you are looking over your left shoulder towards the center of your back. Return your head to center and take a new breath. Then while holding the breath, very slowly turn your head so that you are looking over your right shoulder towards the center of your back. Return your head to center and exhale while slowly lowering your head and shoulders to the floor, forehead again touching the ground. Rest flat on the floor, then repeat this *asana* five or six times.

6. A Simple, Unnamed *Asana*

(For helping cure spinal problems)

This unnamed *asana* was one that I worked out myself for patients with spinal problems, particularly slipped discs.

Stand erect with your feet slightly apart, arms at your side. Now bring arms to shoulder level with your fingertips touching.

Take a deep breath, this is very important, and holding your breath, turn the upper half of your body slowly to the left. Return your body to the center, drop arms to your side and exhale. Repeat exercise turning slowly to the right. Do this exercise three to four times in one session.

This exercise gives flexibility to the whole spine and helps heal a slipped disc in any part of the spinal column. Once I was showing this exercise to a patient and we both heard the disc click back into place.

26
MUDRAS:
Healing Finger Postures

I am a great believer in keeping everything as simple and easy as possible when helping my patients to help themselves.

Many patients find it hard to believe that the very easy yoga finger postures (*mudras*) I detail below, which are a part of the *hatha* yoga discipline, could actually help them. "It just seems too easy, too simple," I'm told by patients unfamiliar with yoga. However, many yoga postures *are* very easy and simple, and many of my patients have continued to stay well by keeping their bodies in balance doing these simple finger postures.

There are literally hundreds of these *mudras*, but I am going to recommend only those I consider the most important for self-healing. Before I describe the actual postures, I'd like to give you some general information about the *mudras* and what they represent.

What *Mudras* Represent

Yoga philosophy pictures the individual as a mini-universe that reflects and duplicates the greater universe. The purpose of doing yoga exercises is to bring the individual's mind and body in harmony with the universal spirit or life force (the *Prana*).

In yogic thinking, our body is made up of five elements — fire or energy; air; sky and ether; earth and water. Each of our five fingers represents one of these elements:

1. The Thumb represents Fire or Energy
2. The Index Finger represents Air
3. The Middle Finger represents Sky and Ether
4. The Ring Finger represents Earth
5. The Little Finger represents Water

In yogic practice, it is believed that whenever there is an imbalance—one element is more active or less active — it creates the disharmony in our system that brings sickness.

In all these *mudras*, Fire (the thumb) must always be included. *Mudras* use a system of *lightly* touching the finger tips, knuckles, or base of the fingers to the thumb — always to the thumb — to produce vital currents. The finger tips contain the ends of certain nerves and if you are sensitive, and as you practice the *mudras* more, you will probably feel the flow of current.

How Long Should You Practice a *Mudra*?

Each of the *mudras* should be done for at least 45 minutes at one time. If you cannot do this, do the *mudra* for two 30-minute periods. Except where specified, the more you can do the *mudra*, the faster you will heal.

Do *Mudras* With Both Hands at The Same Time

Unless otherwise specified, a *mudra* is most effective if you can do it with both hands at the same time. If this is not possible — for example, you are writing, or you are using one hand to hold the book you are reading — do the *mudra* with the hand not in use.

Many people find a good time to do a *mudra* is while walking, watching television, or at the movies. Instead of sitting with your fingers idle, you should try to get into the habit of doing a *mudra*.

I must put in one warning: Most of the *mudras* are for general health and can be done by anyone at any time. One *mudra* — Number 8, the *Shunya Mudra* — should be done only by people with ear troubles.

1. PRANA MUDRA

(For general health and all life-threatening illnesses)

Prana means vital or life force in Sanskrit, and this is the *mudra* I recommend most often for general health.

EDITOR'S NOTE: Sree's hands were photographed to illustrate the mudra postures. In repose they are soft and childishly small, but acquire incredible strength when she uses them in healing.

How you do it: Touch together lightly the tips of the **thumb** (fire or energy), the **ring finger** (earth) and the **little finger** (water).

Why you do it: Bringing these three fingers together makes some special energy start to flow and rejuvenate the whole body. The body's "battery" gets fully charged and it starts to function properly — the special life or vital energy starts flowing inside the body with tremendous force.

I recommend this *mudra* for all patients with life-threatening illnesses, such as cancer, because practicing the *prana mudra* helps activate the immune system. The more it is practiced, the better the result.

I also strongly recommend it for patients with under-activity of the thyroid and several of these patients have achieved remarkable results.

It is also good for patients with various eye weaknesses.

2. JNANA MUDRA

(For improving brain power and memory; insomnia)

The *Jnana Mudra* is called the wisdom posture because *jnana* means knowledge in Sanskrit. In statues of Buddha, this is the hand posture most often shown.

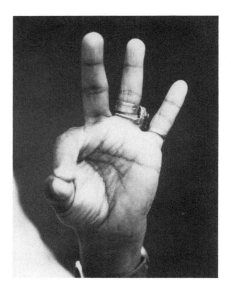

How you do it: In the *Jnana Mudra* you combine Fire with Air by touching together lightly the tip of the **thumb** to the tip of the **index finger**. This is a beneficial finger exercise that everyone should do.

Why you do it: This mudra increases the flow of blood to the brain and for this reason, it helps increase brain power and memory retention.

It can be useful for sufferers of insomnia; here I speak from personal experience, as I have cured my own insomnia using this *mudra*.

It is also the posture that generates harmony, peace, bliss and knowledge of the mysterious universe beyond our conscious knowledge.

3. BAYAU MUDRA

(For joint pains)

Bayau means air in Sanskrit. This *mudra* is designed to help the vital air in our body to flow properly.

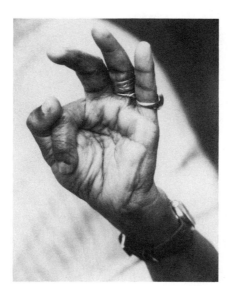

How you do it: The **thumb** (fire) and the **index finger** (air) are again used, but in a different position. The index finger lightly touches and presses the base of the thumb. The thumb then curls over and lightly presses the knuckle of the index finger.

Why you do it: This is an excellent *mudra* for helping rid the body of joint pains like rheumatism and arthritis, even paralysis. It will not help for pains like earaches or stomachache, which are not related to the vital air.

For the best results, alternate with practice of the *Prana Mudra* (see *Mudra* No. 1 above).

4. PRITHVI MUDRA

(For increased bodily energy and flexibility of mind)

In Sanskrit, *prithvi* means earth. When fire touches earth, the dynamo of the body starts charging.

How you do it: Touch the tip of the **thumb** (fire or energy) to the tip of the **ring finger** (earth).

Why you do it: This *mudra* helps when there is a weakness in the body due to a lack of vitamins. By the renewed flow of energy, the part of the body lacking nourishment, starts getting it.

This *mudra* also helps to promote flexibility of mind; one becomes more open-minded, less obstinate, and more open to the ideas of others. This is also the *mudra* whose practice leads to the experience of different kinds of bliss.

5. SURYA MUDRA

(To rid the body of lethargy)

Surya means sun in Sanskrit. In this posture the **thumb** and **ring finger** are used to create a different kind of electrical impulse.

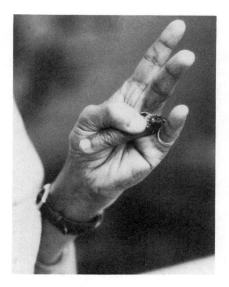

How you do it: First, touch the tip of the **ring finger** (earth) to the base of the **thumb** (fire). Then curl the thumb over the knuckle of the ring finger.

Why you do it: This is used when the body feels heavy or lethargic. It promotes lightness and, though this may sound strange, one starts to acquire mystical power.

6. VARUN MUDRA

(For kidney problems and impure blood)

Varun means water in Sanskrit and this *mudra* is designed to rectify all the problems related to lack of sufficient water in the body, such as dryness or blood impurities.

How you do it: This *mudra* is very easy to do. One touches the tip of the **little finger** (water) to the tip of the **thumb** (fire or energy).

Why you do it: Our bodies are made up of seventy percent fluid. If one does not have enough water in our bodies, the system gets out of balance. I frequently recommend this *mudra* to patients with kidney problems, stiffness and impure blood.

7. LINGA MUDRA

(For any kind of chest weakness)

This *mudra* uses all the fingers of both hands and generates heat throughout the entire body.

How you do it: Place both palms together. Then clasp the fingers of the right hand with the left hand in such a manner that **you keep only the left thumb erect**. The thumb and index finger of the right hand clasp the left thumb tightly, then clasp the other fingers.

Why you do it: When one feels cold, doing this *mudra* will bring warmth to the whole body. It is also excellent for those with chronic coughs and colds. Done with patience, it will achieve wonderful results.

8. SHUNYA MUDRA

(For ear problems)

WARNING: This *mudra* should be used *only* by people with *ear problems*. People who do not have ear problems should not do it because it could lead to blockage of the ears. Also, for this *mudra*, you do *not* use both hands.

If the problem is in **the right ear**, one does the *mudra* only with **the right hand**.

If the problem is in **the left ear**, one does the *mudra* only with **the left hand**.

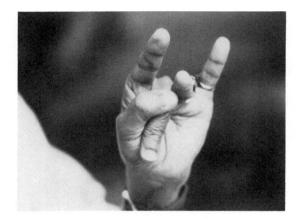

How you do it: This *mudra* uses the **thumb** (fire or energy) with the **middle finger** (sky or ether). The middle finger lightly touches the base of the thumb and the thumb curls over and presses the knuckle of the middle finger.

Patients with ear problems should do this *mudra* as often as possible, for 45 minutes at one time, or for two, 30-minute intervals. The more often one does this *mudra*, the better the result.

I describe in Chapter 22 how using this *mudra* helped a child of five, the son of a famous eye surgeon, to regain his hearing when all the doctors had told his father that the child would be partially deaf for life.

9. APANA VAYU MUDRA or MRITA-SANJIBANI MUDRA

(For any kind of heart problem)

This *mudra* is helpful in improving all heart weakness.

How you do it: Join the tip of the **index finger** (air) to the base of the **thumb** (fire). Then lightly place the tips of your **middle and ring fingers** (sky and earth) on the tip of your thumb.

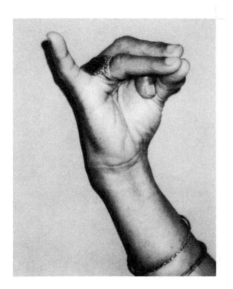 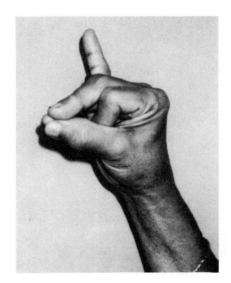

Why you do it: While helpful for any kind of heart problem, it is also claimed that practicing this *mudra* can even prevent a heart attack. I cannot vouch for that myself, but the patient with symptoms of a heart attack who is waiting for his doctor, or who is on the way to the hospital, could certainly practice it to calm the nerves.

10. APANA MUDRA

(For urinary obstructions **not** due to prostate problems)

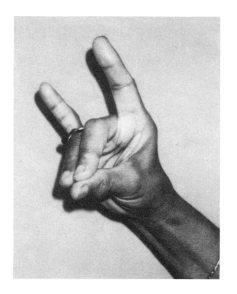 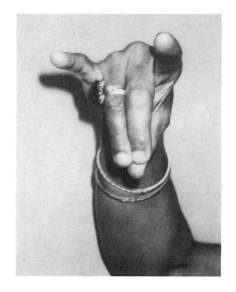

How you do it: Join together the tip of the **thumb** (fire) to the tips of the **middle and ring fingers** (sky and earth).

Why you do it: Patients with urinary obstructions that prevent them passing water (**not** due to prostate gland problems) will be helped to pass water if they practice this *mudra*. It is also recommended for diabetic urinary problems.

This *mudra* is also useful in opening a blocked nose and in opening the pores of the skin to allow the patient to perspire and cleanse the body of impurities. This *mudra* also helps in self-realization.

NOTE: Although there are many yoga institutions where *mudras* are taught and written about, I first read about these *mudras* in the writings of Acharya Keshar Dev. A number of his books have been translated into English and are available from the Vivekanada Yogashram Hospital, Patparganj Road (Khureji), Delhi-51, INDIA.

27
USING COLOR TO HEAL

Color meditation is the ancient yogic practice of visualizing color to revitalize and heal the body. Before I describe the theory and practice of color meditation, I will briefly describe my technique for those readers not familiar with meditation. The colors visualized follow the order of the colors of the rainbow, the universal and uplifting symbol of hope.

How to Meditate

I recommend six specific points of technique for meditation or relaxation response.

1. In preparing to meditate the important thing to remember is that you keep your spine straight. If you can do it comfortably, sit cross-legged on the floor or a hard surface, keeping the spine straight. If you can't do this comfortably, don't worry, just sit on an armchair or a straight chair, whichever you prefer, but remember to sit erect.
2. Close your eyes.
3. Deeply relax all your muscles, beginning at your feet and progressing up to your head.
4. Breathing through your nose, equalize your breathing. You do this by breathing in to the count of 7; holding your breath for the count of 1; exhaling to the count of 7 and holding again for the count of 1.

5. When you are breathing comfortably in this rhythm of 7:1:7:1, start saying "one" or "om" silently to yourself each time you breathe out. Do this for 10 or 20 minutes. (I believe the word "one" is as good as any transcendental (TM) *mantra* for the purpose of meditation or relaxation response.) However, if you are in a place where you can say "om" out loud, the vibration of the word itself on your spine has a healing effect.

6. When you finish, sit quietly for several minutes, first with your eyes closed, then open.

The Theory of Color Meditation

In yogic philosophy, each of the seven colors of the rainbow is associated with one of the seven *chakras*, the invisible energy centers along the spine. *Chakra* means wheel in Sanskrit and each *chakra* is imagined as a lotus-shaped, whirling wheel or vortex that can be "opened" by the power of thought to draw into the body the energy of the *prana* or the life force. This *prana* is then broken up on the wheel of the *chakra*, and the energy is distributed back to our bodies through the web of energy streams radiating from each *chakra*.

In terms of our physical body, each *chakra* is associated with an endocrine gland that governs specific bodily functions. When you visualize the color associated with the *chakra*, the energy this generates helps heal that particular area of the body.

In this section I shall describe each of the *chakras*, the color associated with it, and the area of the body it governs:

First Chakra: The Muladhara

Location: At the base of the spinal column.
Meditation color: Rose Red.
Element: Earth. It is the electric force of creation.
Associated endocrine gland: The gonads.

Meditating on this point of focus leads to the mastery of desire, envy and anger. This *chakra* also governs the sense of smell and stimulates our knowledge of speech.

The *muladhara* is also visualized as the source of the *kundalini shakti* (serpent power), pictured as a serpent coiled around the base of the spine. When this power is properly activated by meditation, it rises through the other *chakras* or lotuses in the spine and finally unites with the thousand-petalled lotus in the crown of the head called the SAHASRARA. This is the aim of all dedicated yogis — slowly to awaken one after another of the lotuses until union with the divine is achieved.

Second Chakra: The Svadisthana

Location: At the root of the genitals.
Meditation color: Orange-red.
Element: Water.
Associated endocrine gland: The adrenals.

Mediation on the orange-red color helps control the functioning of the kidneys and vitalizes the whole body, including the legs.

Third Chakra: The Manipura

Location: Opposite the navel. Often called the "navel" lotus.
Meditation color: Yellow.
Element: Fire
Associated endocrine gland: The pancreas.

Meditation on the color yellow floods yellow rays into the abdomen to stimulate the pancreas and help the liver, gall bladder and the whole nervous system.

It is a very important meditation center because it is also the focus for the solar plexus, the reservoir of psychic power.

Fourth Chakra: The Anahata

Location: On the spine, opposite the heart. Often called the "heart" lotus.
Meditation color: Green.
Element: Air.
Associated endocrine gland: The thymus.

The green color of the *Anahata* combines the yellow of the *chakra* below with the sky-blue of the *chakra* above. This union symbolizes this *chakra*'s central role in transforming the energy of the lower *chakras* into the higher degrees of consciousness. In the physical body, this is paralleled by the heart's power to purify the blood and vitalize the system.

For this meditation, you should visualize a steady green light in the center of the heart. Meditating on the color green is particularly valuable for patients with any kind of heart or circulation problems.

Fifth Chakra: The Vishuddha

Location: At the base of the throat.
Meditation color: Sky-blue.
Element: The ether.
Associated endocrine gland: The thyroid.

Meditating on this sky-blue color — which may not be easy for the novice to achieve — brings a feeling of cooling calm and peace as the energy surges upward into the throat region. This meditation affects the lungs, bronchial areas, the alimentary canal, and the power of speech.

Sixth Chakra: The Ajna

Location: Between the eyebrows, sometimes called the "third eye."
Meditation color: Indigo-blue.
Associated endocrine gland: The pineal gland.

The *Ajna* and the seventh *chakra*, the *Sahasrara*, are associated with both the pineal and the pituitary glands. Meditation on indigo-blue will help problems of the lower brain, the ears, and eyes.

It is believed that the yogi who meditates upon the *Ajna chakra* as he approaches death will dissolve into and be united with the supreme being at the moment the soul departs the body.

Seventh Chakra: The Sahasrara

Location: The crown of the head. The *Sahasrara* is imagined as the transcendental point of focus that governs and transforms the energy of the six lower *chakras*.

Meditation color: Violet-white.
Associated endocrine gland: The pituitary.

The *Sahasrara* governs the upper brain and the right eye. It is the meeting point of opposite polarities: Shiva and Shakti, male and female, electric and magnetic, solar and lunar. Above all, it is the transcendental point of focus, the ultimate aim of meditation.

Practicing Color Meditation

You are prepared to meditate, breathing comfortably in the regular rhythm of 7:1:7:1. Now imagine you are inhaling the **rose-red** color of the first *chakra*. Visualize the rose-red as pouring into your body from the sun, spreading throughout your whole body, bringing it strength and vitality. Relax and let it flood over you.

Next, visualize the color **orange-red**. It, too, represents the sun in all its healing energy.

Next imagine the color **yellow** to stimulate the pancreas gland, the stomach and liver.

Now try to visualize **green**. particularly important for any weakness of the heart.

Now try to see **sky-blue**. Don't be discouraged if it becomes increasingly difficult to visualize the colors of the higher *chakras*. The blue and indigo-blue color visualizations bring a feeling of cooling and spiritual healing.

Finally, for the most advanced color meditation, there is the **violet-white** of the seventh *chakra* that brings purity of mind, serenity and peace.

By meditation and proper breathing exercises, we make the mind finer, and the finer the instrument, the greater the power. Our soaring thoughts become the healing thought for the whole universe. With the power of the mind we can conquer fears of illness, old age, even of death. At the end of our earthly journey, when the time will come for our union with God, we will leave our bodies peacefully:

Everything must have emanated from the Absolute, and everything must return to it.

28
USING SOUND TO HEAL

Sound is used in yoga both to vitalize the body and to prepare the mind for meditation.

I have found *The Ten-Point Way to Health** by the Rajah of Aundh an invaluable guide to the use of sound in healing, and as a way to maintain my own health. It is unfortunate that his excellent book — which also includes a program of exercises — is now out of print.

I recommend following a daily regimen in which the following seven sounds are practised: the mystic syllable OM (the *pranava*) followed in turn by each of the six sounds known as the *bija mantras* — HRAM, HRIM, HRUM, HRAIM, HRAUM and HRAH.

How the Sounds Help to Heal

The author explains why the loud and clear repetition of these particular sounds, used by yogis for hundreds of years, has healing value:

- OM — pronounced O-O-O, M-M-M — vibrates through the spine to vitalize the whole body.
- The "H" in the six *bija mantras* proceeds from the heart, making the heart beat more vigorously and helping in the purification of the blood.

---

* *The Ten-Point Way to Health* by the Rajah of Aundh, D.B. Taraporevala Sons and Co. Pvt. Ltd., Treasure House of Books, 210 Dr. Dadabhai Naoroji Rd., Bombay 1, India

- The "M" sound at the end of five of the six *bija mantras* also helps purify the blood when the breath is inhaled and exhaled through the nose.
  Also, by terminating each of the five *mantras* with the long "M" sound, the nose and windpipe are kept healthy.
- The "R" sound in the *mantras* is considered to be almost as important as OM. By uttering the consonant "R," the tip of the tongue strikes the front palate and vibrates the brain.
  Thus, by uttering each of the syllables in the first five *mantras*, the heart, windpipe and brain are all invigorated.

Note: In reciting the *bija mantras*, one breathes in deeply through the nose, then opens the mouth for the "H" sound and closes it for the "M" sound. Remember, all the sounds are *long*.

How to Say the Sounds

- **OM:** OM, which preceeds each of the six *bija mantras* — is pronounced O-O-O — M-M-M to rhyme with "home." Open the mouth for the O-O-O and close it for the M-M-M.
- **HRAM** is pronounced H-R-A-A-A-M-M-M to rhyme with "calm". The continuous long "A" in HRAM strengthens the rib cage, purges the alimentary canal and cleanses and stimulates the upper portion of the lungs. Thus this *mantra* can help in curing asthma and bronchitis.
- **HRIM:** The long vowel "I" is prounced "EE" to rhyme with "seem." Saying HRIM stimulates the action of the throat, palate, the nose, and the upper part of the heart. It also clears the respiratory and digestive passages of phlegm.
- **HRUM:** The long vowel "U" is pronounced to rhyme with "room." This sound stimulates the liver, spleen, stomach and intestines, and reduces the abdomen. It is particularly important for women suffering from chronic diseases of the lower abdomen.
- **HRAIM:** The vowels "AI" are pronounced to rhyme with "time." This stirs up the kidneys and acts as a diuretic.

- **HRAUM:** The vowels "AU" are pronounced "OU," as in "round." This sound helps the rectum and anus to function normally.
- **HRAH:** HRAH is said as "HURRAH," and acts to vibrate the chest and throat.

To sum up:

The Sound	Rhymes With	Areas Afffected/Helped
OM	"home"	Spinal cord, a general restorative.
HRAM	"calm"	Lungs: helps with asthma and bronchitis.
HRIM	"seem"	Throat, palate, nose, upper part of heart. Clears respiratory and digestive passages.
HRUM	"room"	Liver, spleen, stomach and intestines.
HRAIM	"time"	Kidneys.
HRAUM	Au as "ou"in "round"	Rectum and anus.
HRAH	as in "hurrah"	Vibrates chest and throat.

There is no mandatory number of times to say these mantras. However, one should say them least 10 times — always preceeded by OM — but the more times you say them the better.

INDEX

Page numbers in bold refer to remedies for the listed condition.